Samuel Fosso

Introduction by Christine Barthe

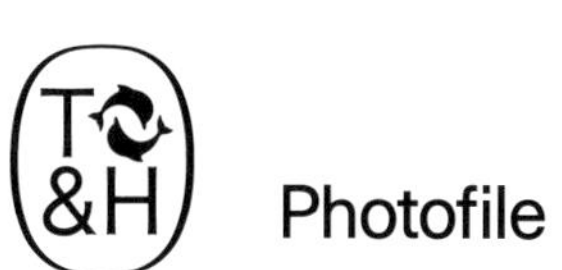

Photofile

Samuel Fosso: pictures of his lives

To explore a body of work composed of self-portraits implies a constant interplay between the biographical and the photographic. These elements could be said to represent the two sides that make up Samuel Fosso's images. But they are not enough to account for the complexity of an oeuvre built up over forty years by this unclassifiable artist. Since the beginning of his career in 1974, Fosso has constructed a body of work that is unique and the result of a remarkable journey, one whose development we shall be attempting to understand better. The context of the late 1960s is vital to pinpointing the circumstances in which a young man once destined to become a healer, then a shoemaker, was able, contrary to all expectations, to become a major figure in 21st-century photography.

The artist talks openly about his virtual lack of childhood: born in 1962 in Cameroon to Nigerian parents, in early infancy he suffered from paralysis of the arms and legs. Accompanied by his mother, he was cared for by his grandfather, a healer, in Nigeria. Forced with his parents to seek refuge in the jungle at the outbreak of the Biafran War (1967–70), he was isolated from the rest of his family. After his mother's death, he was raised by his grandparents until his uncle, who lived in Bangui (Central African Republic), took him in, in 1972, to train him in his craft of shoemaking. With this challenging start in life, the artist says that he was not a child deemed worthy of being photographed on account of his disability and that there is therefore no portrait of him at the age of three months, as was customary at the time. He sees in this a key element of his practice of self-portraiture:

'When you ask me why I privilege self-portraits, I believe the answer is rooted in the condition of my life, and the meaning of self-representation… Making them gave me the opportunity to engage in my own biography: going back to when I was a child, when no one thought I was a desirable child to photograph.'[1]

Fosso began his professional life extremely young, when in 1974 he persuaded the Nigerian owner of the Tonatus photography studio in Bangui to take him on as an apprentice. After a few months, he was given permission to take photographs and he immediately began to make self-portraits in addition to his work as a commercial photographer. An early image shows him seated, turning towards the camera in a pose that is artfully casual (ill. 1). In September 1975, at the age of thirteen, he started his own business, Studio Photo Nationale. Numerous self-portraits followed in the subsequent years. In order to take them, the photographer used the last few inches of film left over from his commercial commissions and gradually built up a repertoire of attitudes, poses and gestures, along with some recognizable outfits. Nowadays he draws attention to the torn garments of his early images and can date pictures from certain notable accessories, such as the now famous platform boots bought in Nigeria in 1977, in which he poses like the Cameroonian-Nigerian singer Prince Nico Mbarga on the cover of his hit record *Sweet Mother*.

1974–78: 'I was living out a series of ideas about myself'[2]

During this period, Fosso's self-portraits fell within the sphere of the strictly personal and were not considered artistic works. Fosso has often noted this apparent paradox by explaining that the pictures were mainly intended for his grandmother in Nigeria, and that he was not then aware of being an artist.[3] However, looking at the images today, they reveal a true skill, a style that borrows from multiple codes, expertly recombined. But, above all, there is an obvious and imperative need to create images. In search of artists driven by this need, the photographer Bernard Descamps met Samuel Fosso in 1993 while he was organizing the first Bamako Biennale, which took place the following year. When Fosso showed him his commercial work, Descamps asked him: 'Do you have any other images, ones you take for yourself?'[4] Thus the black-and-white images were unearthed, some twenty years after they were taken; Fosso already considered them ancient but had carefully preserved them for his children.[5]

Fosso won first prize at the festival in 1994, paving the way for a career in which the artisan made way for the author. This defining encounter showed that to find their audience, these images needed a context – the Bamako Biennale – and an attentive observer to notice them: Bernard Descamps.[6] Aside from the sheer number of amassed photographs, the most striking feature of these images was the personality of Samuel Fosso, his ability to seize any opportunity to become a new person, to play a new role.

Tati (1997): a springboard

In fact, the Bamako Biennale proved to be a decisive turning point, bringing images originally intended for personal use to a broad public audience. Fosso subsequently exhibited at the Centre National de la Photographie in Paris in 1995, then in 1996 took part in the group show 'In/sight: African Photographers, 1940 to the Present' at the Guggenheim Museum in New York. He seemed entirely nonplussed by this sudden fame. When, in 1997, he was invited by the French department store Tati to take part in an event alongside Seydou Keïta and Malick Sidibé, the young photographer saw an opportunity to distinguish himself and sought a way of not simply reproducing the imagery expected from a portrait studio.[7] He decided to work in colour and to use Tati's resources to access large quantities of clothing and accessories. He shot a dozen or so self-portraits in which he played a range of socio-professional roles, designed to focus attention on others rather than himself: the businessman, the golfer, the bourgeois woman; or stereotypical characters reminiscent of extras on a film set: the rocker, the pirate, the sailor, the lifeguard. Two more surprising figures were to acquire significant notoriety, on account of their political implications. These images bore long titles that sounded more like statements: 'The Liberated American Woman of the 70s' ('La femme américaine libérée des années 70') shows us the bold, joyful and carefully composed image of a woman played by Samuel Fosso with confidence and ease, and without a hint of irony.

'The Chief (the One who Sold Africa to the Colonists)', or 'Le Chef (celui qui a vendu l'Afrique aux colons)', is a scathing portrait that borrows from various picture sources, including portraits of Mobutu Sese Seko, former president of the Democratic Republic of the Congo. The *Tati* series showed Fosso's desire to reinvent himself and reject simple categorization, but also his ability to carefully integrate the skills of professionals such as prop makers, stylists and make-up artists, with whom he would work on future occasions.

The success of the colourful and appealing *Tati* images might have resulted in the artist being tempted to embark on an endless variety of role-playing games. But the creation of *Mémoire d'un ami* ('Memory of a Friend') led him towards output that was much more direct, and in black and white.

From dream lives to real lives: *Mémoire d'un ami* (2000) and
***Le Rêve de mon grand-père* (2003)**

An atypical and lesser-known series, *Mémoire d'un ami* is probably one of the most directly autobiographical. It reconstructs a painful scene experienced by the artist in Bangui in 1997, when a neighbour and friend, Tala, was attacked and killed in his home by militia. During an artist's residency in Cameroon, Fosso created a series of nine images in which he appears alone and frightened inside his home, shielding himself from an invisible aggressor. The images form a sequence covering several locations (in the bedroom, at the door, on the bed) but individually remain quite enigmatic.[8] The photographs showing Fosso reclining on the bed recall – and at the same time distort – the subject of the female odalisque in art. His naked body evades the iconography of eroticism in order to evoke fragility, vulnerability and solitude at first hand.[9]

It is interesting to draw a parallel with another series with autobiographical connections, *Le Rêve de mon grand-père* ('My Grandfather's Dream'), created a few years later. In this series, Fosso acts out an initiation scene. The shots were taken in a temporary studio and the work featured his nephews. The images borrow from ethnographic iconography, deconstructing its gestures and poses. However, they form a complex reconstruction in which the artist acts out a scene that should have happened in his life: his healer grandfather had wanted to pass on his knowledge to him. Staging his own initiation into the profession of healer, Fosso uses photography to create a scene of family transmission that is now impossible. He could not be a healer but became a photographer, and because he is a photographer, he can imagine himself as a healer. *Le Rêve de mon grand-père* is probably the most metaphorical of his series and also delves into the roots of his childhood, depicting an impossible event that has been made possible through art.

Approaching History

In 2008, the *African Spirits* series provided a fresh impetus. After reinventing new selves for himself (1970s), trying his hand at role play (*Tati*), and reconstructing the link with his grandfather through images (*Le Rêve de mon grand-père*), Fosso decided to embody major historical figures, African and African-American emblems of the struggles for independence and civil rights, and significant artists. The photographer was firmly rooted in his times, he was receptive to geopolitical events, and, while history was manifest in his images first and foremost through experience (*Mémoire d'un ami*), with *African Spirits* it emerged in a radically different way. One should note the context of the year 2008, which saw Barack Obama accede to the presidency of the United States, as well as the title of Obama's autobiography, *Dreams from my Father* (1995), subsequently published in French under the title *Les Rêves de mon père*. Fosso also cited his visit to the exhibition 'The Short Century' as one of the factors that led him to create *African Spirits*.

African Spirits was a project that required an entire team (make-up artist, stylist, assistant photographer) and substantial resources, including a large-format view camera that made massive enlargements possible. Fosso chose black and white for the prints, embedding the dual historical nature of his images in a photographic code from the past. In this series, he played, interpreted and, above all, reincarnated well-known personalities: Martin Luther King, Aimé Césaire, Angela Davis, Patrice Lumumba, as well as Miles Davis and Seydou Keïta. He reconstructed existing photographs, putting himself in the place of the historical figure: for example, the portrait of Malcolm X by Richard Avedon, newspaper images of Tommie Smith raising his fist, and the official portrait of the Ethiopian emperor Haile Selassie. Fosso emphasized the relationship between these prominent African and Black figures and the history of slavery: 'I see slavery as connected to all these questions of freedom, liberation, colonialism, and power. To me, slavery was the source, and I wanted to deal with it in a really deep way… And these figures were committed to the idea of freedom for black people in order to reclaim their culture and human dignity. This was the underlying concept of *African Spirits*.' He added: 'It was always my wish that these images would appear in museums – where images of these figures are completely absent – and therefore they would be remembered in the future by children who visit these institutions.'[10]

In *African Spirits*, Fosso once again reveals his talent as an actor, his ability to embody real people. He does it with a fresh awareness of his role as spokesman, now possible thanks to his status and his position within the artistic spectrum: 'If artists don't take advantage of this opportunity, slavery, Black history will never be told… I am an artist. I am well known. Now it's up to me to reveal those who are hidden.'[11] The search for identity that had been discernible in his work up to this point now took on a new dimension, with this opportunity to act on behalf of others, in the name of a collective, and to place himself within a shared history.

He continued to play the role of conduit in works that followed. In *Emperor of Africa* (2013) and *Black Pope* (2017), the artist-actor's astonishing powers of metamorphosis emerged in his virtuoso reappropriation of a highly codified iconography of propaganda and in the irrefutable embodiment of a Black pope, respectively.

SIXSIXSIX (2016): a fragile monument

SIXSIXSIX was the first work to take the form of an installation. It was a unique piece, consisting of 666 Polaroid images in 24 × 19 cm format. For this large-scale production, an entire team was assembled in Paris between late 2015 and early 2016 to find the materials and resources to develop it. The project required several trial runs to establish a process that would produce images with a sufficiently even tone. For the self-portraits, Fosso posed without make-up or visible clothing in front of the large-format camera. The camera captured his face in close-up, like a passport photo. The monumental nature of the finished installation[12] provided a striking contrast with the apparent simplicity of each image.

SIXSIXSIX followed a painful period in Fosso's life. He experienced the turmoil of the Central African Republic Civil War, and in February 2014 his studio in Bangui was looted by militias. Although some of the archives were saved by the intervention of photojournalists Jérôme Delay and Marcus Bleasdale, the destruction was almost complete. The artist devised SIXSIXSIX against this backdrop, the number in its title being a reference to the devil. The results appear to be simply shot: no artifice, no transformation. Fosso's bare features are captured in 666 different expressions, creating a confrontation with the viewer that is rather dizzying. The colour and brightness of the Polaroids gave the images a highly pictorial look, but each photograph was a snapshot that interacts with the viewer in a very direct, raw way. The difference in scale between faces that were life-size, but repeated across a distance of almost 100 metres, produced a monumental work that was nevertheless intimate. The work brought viewers into a direct relationship with the portraits, creating a mirroring effect – the quantitative excess contrasting with the restraint of the composition. The impact of the work lay in its formal qualities and the way it achieved a kind of universality by referring to personal experiences of sadness: 'The life we live changes like the light of day. There is suffering, there is joy, there are moments when one is happy, and moments when one is sad. Moments when one laughs, becomes angry… that's the way life is… As for me, I have seen life like this.'[13]

It was an eloquent work – more to be perceived than to be deciphered – that radiated an obvious truth. In doing so, it achieved the aim of the artist, who said: 'I want to note that what I am interested in communicating with my images is, simply, the truth.'[14] This close communication with viewers echoed the path followed by Fosso, who had proven himself able to reinvent his own methods of creation and ways of interacting with the world. Questioned about his working methods, he explained: 'When I have an idea and an inspiration, I simply do my job. Once I am finished with a project, I tend to withdraw a bit; I become both shy and afraid because I know the job is not finished… I am first and foremost interested in the viewer's response to my ideas, and only when I have presented the work in public do I lose my shyness and fear.'[15] The unveiling he performed in SIXSIXSIX certainly demanded a level of trust with the public.

If we go back to the circumstances in which Fosso's works were produced, we can see differences between the limited means of his early years, which could increase considerably (*Tati*) but also return to less elaborate forms (*Mémoire d'un ami*). Fosso exercises freedom of choice when it comes to projects: working alone or with a team, in Africa or in France. Represented since 2000 by Jean Marc Patras, he has benefited from significant resources for certain projects, without restricting himself to a single way of working. Asked about a perceived increase in complexity in his working methods, he replied: 'If I have the opportunity, the creative decisions are not difficult for me. I always have the ideas for creation.'[16] The question of resources becomes relatively less important for an artist who maintains creative freedom. In 2021, Fosso revisited his early self-portraits in the series *Fosso Fashion 2021*.[17] These are fashion shots in which the interior of his first studio is recreated. He poses as a dandy, with a gravity far removed from his youthful self-portraits, with no trace of nostalgia. Time has passed and his body of work has grown. We can measure the distance between the early self-portraits made for himself and his immediate family, and the scope of works such as *African Spirits* and SIXSIXSIX, in which it is possible to perceive a certain sense of completion and an apparent awareness of the responsibility of the artist.

Christine Barthe

Notes

1   Okwui Enwezor (ed.), *Samuel Fosso: Autoportrait*, New York: Walther Collection; Göttingen: Steidl, 2020, pp. 12 & 18.

2   Okwui Enwezor, 2020, p. 18.

3   This is mentioned in a number of interviews, notably Okwui Enwezor, 2020, and 'Les vies de Samuel Fosso: une conversation avec Yves Chatap', *Contemporary And*, 2017: https://contemporaryand.com/fr/magazines/the-lives-of-samuel-fosso-a-conversation-with-yves-chatap/

4   Private conversation, September 2021.

5   'Il n'y a pas de présent sans passé', in Clément Chéroux, *La voix du voir: les grands entretiens de la fondation Henri Cartier-Bresson*, Paris: Xavier Barral, 2019, p. 217.

6   For specific information on the role played by Bernard Descamps, see Clément Chéroux, 2019.

7   Okwui Enwezor, 2020, p. 16, and 'Samuel Fosso' in Christine Barthe (ed.), 'À toi appartient le regard et […] la liaison infinie entre les choses', Paris: Musée du Quai Branly – Jacques Chirac; Arles: Actes Sud, 2020, p. 75.

8   See in particular the image in which Samuel Fosso poses with a mirror.

9   On the question of nudity, see 'Il n'y a pas de présent sans passé', in Clément Chéroux, 2019, pp. 214–15.

10   Okwui Enwezor, 2020, p. 19.

11   Christine Barthe, 2020, p. 75.

12   Displayed in its entirety in 2020 in the exhibition 'À toi appartient le regard et […] la liaison infinie entre les choses', the piece can exist in various forms.

13   Interview with Samuel Fosso by Christine Barthe, on the occasion of the exhibition 'À toi appartient le regard et […] la liaison infinie entre les choses', 1 October 2020, Musée du Quai Branly – Jacques Chirac, Paris: https://www.youtube.com/watch?v=XzT1ha33Kac.

14   Okwui Enwezor, 2020, p. 20.

15   Okwui Enwezor, 2020, p. 20.

16   Okwui Enwezor, 2020, p. 17.

17   Produced in Paris for the magazine *A Magazine Curated by Grace Wales Bonner*, 2021, echoing the series *Fosso Fashion* shot for *Vogue Hommes* in Bangui in 1999–2000.

1. *70's Lifestyle* series, 1974.

First self-portrait taken at the Tonatus studio.

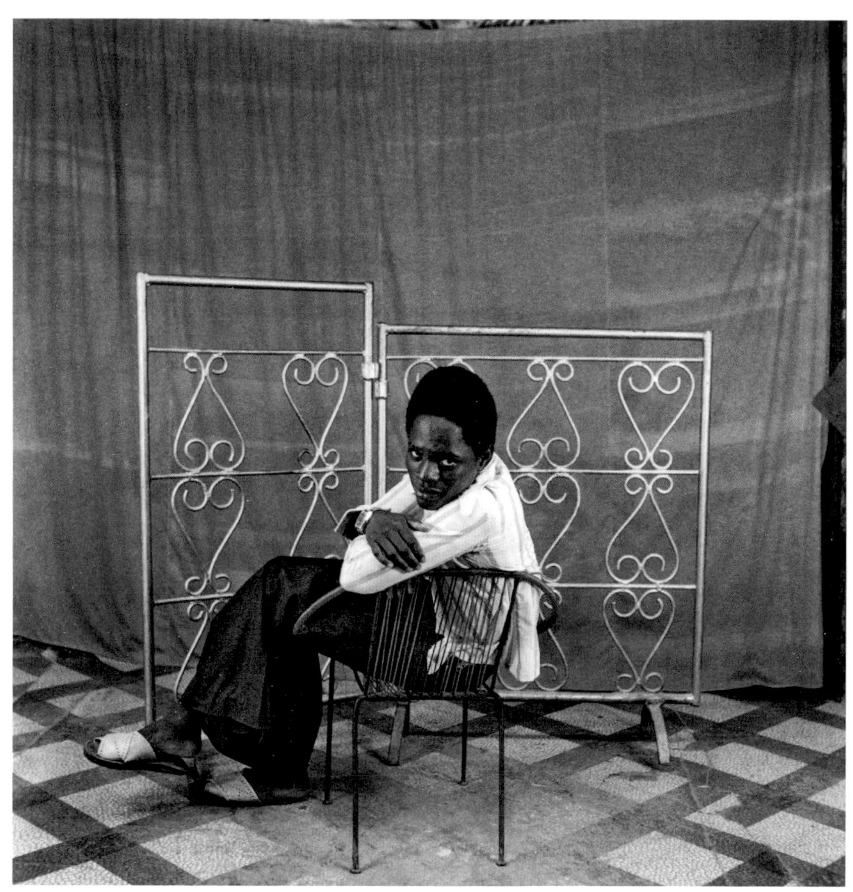

2–4. *70's Lifestyle* series, 1975.

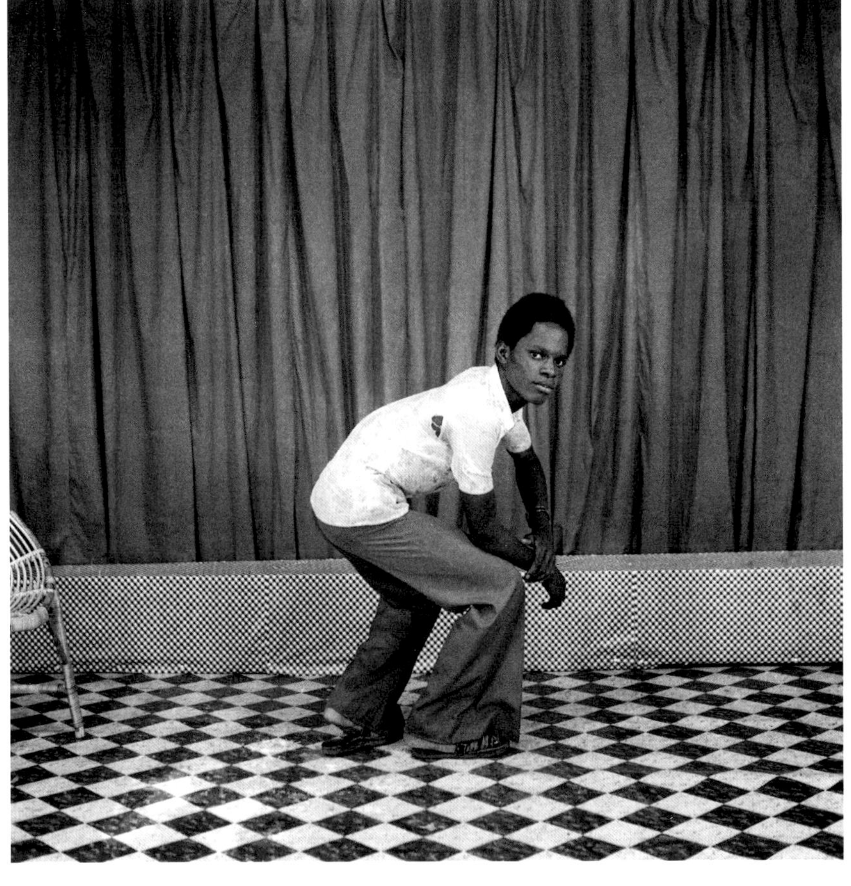

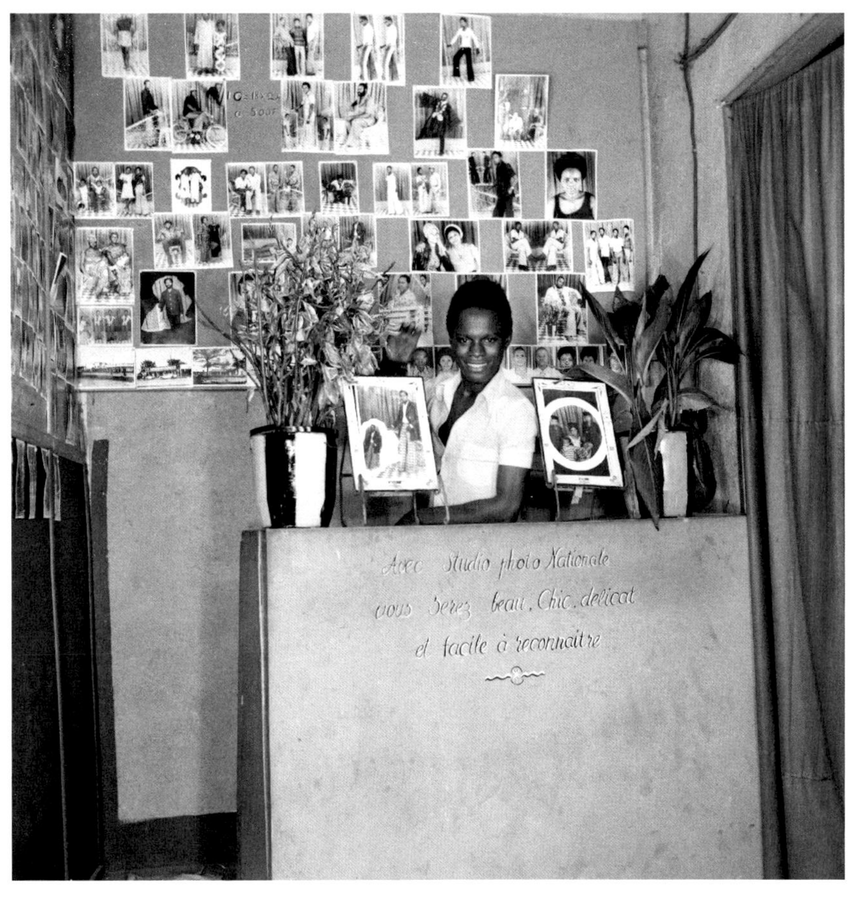
Avec studio photo Nationale
vous serez beau. Chic. delicat
et facile à reconnaître

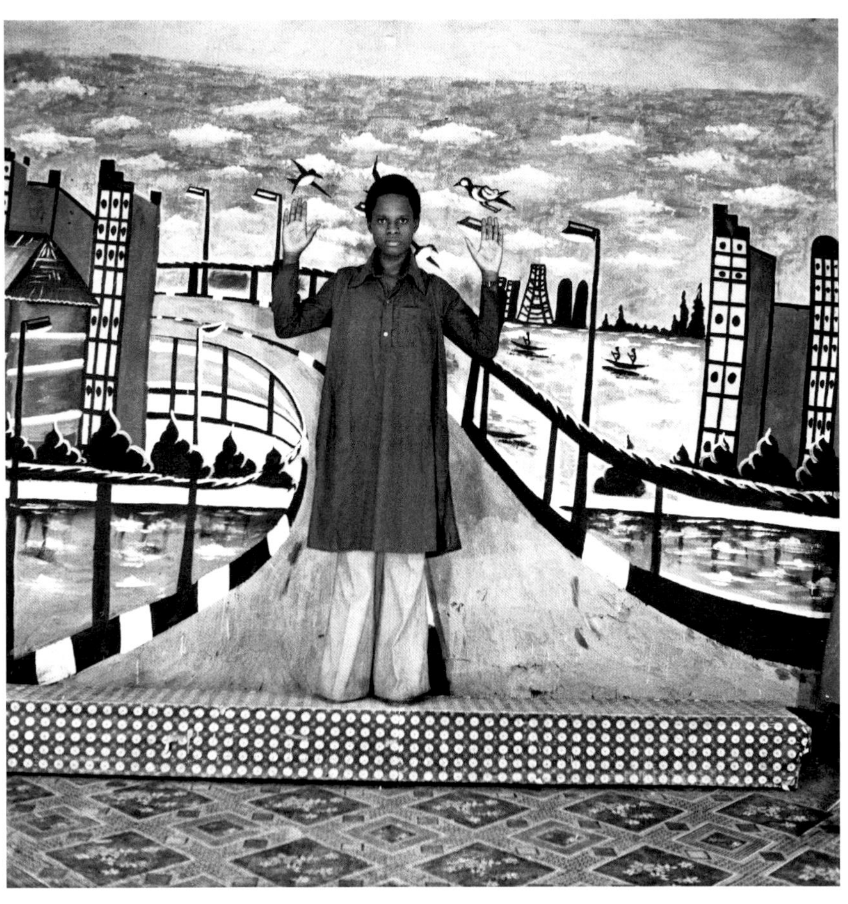

5. *70's Lifestyle* series, 1976.

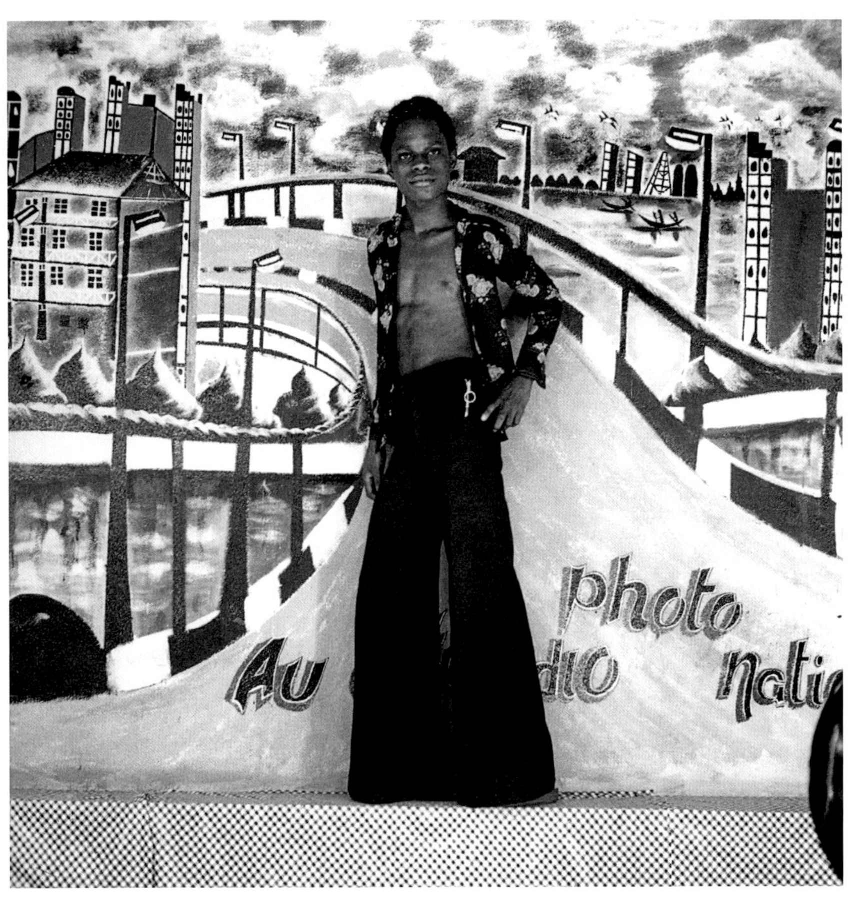

photo
Au   dio   nati

6. *70's Lifestyle* series, 1975–76.

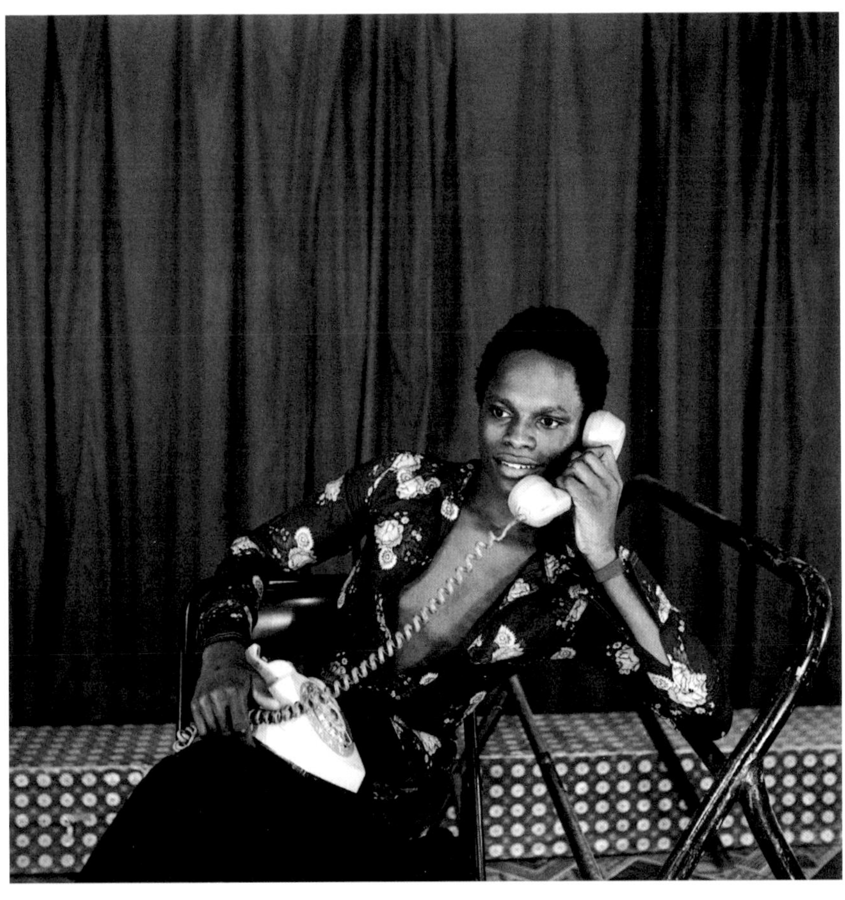

7. *70's Lifestyle* series, 1976–77.

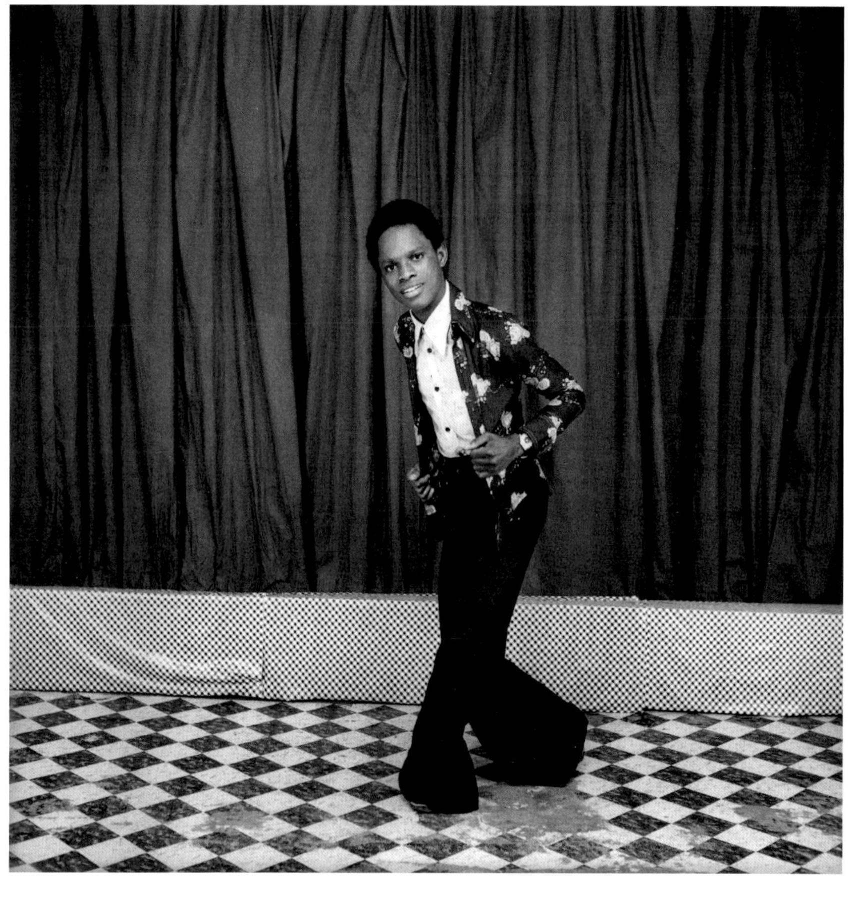

8–11. *70's Lifestyle* series, 1976.

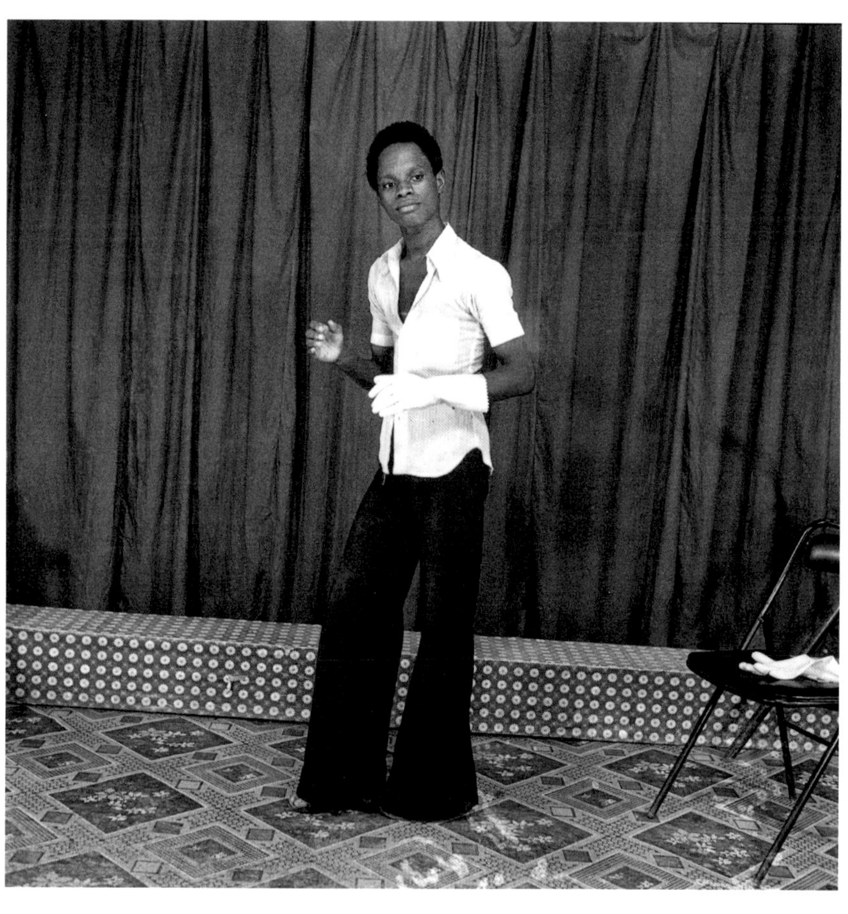

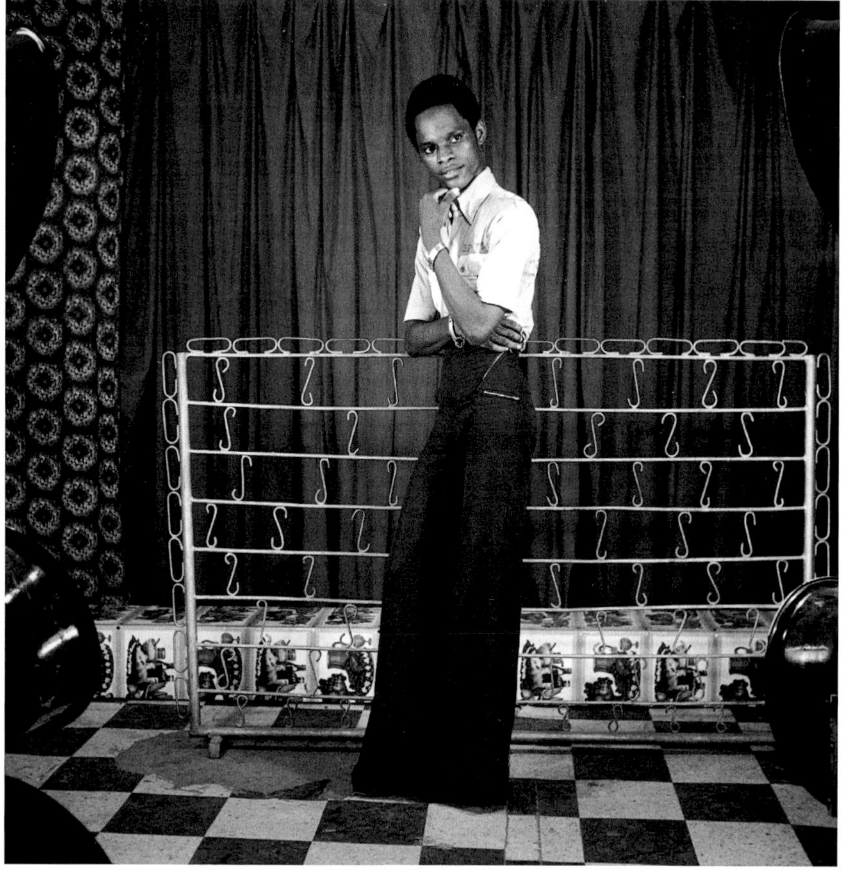

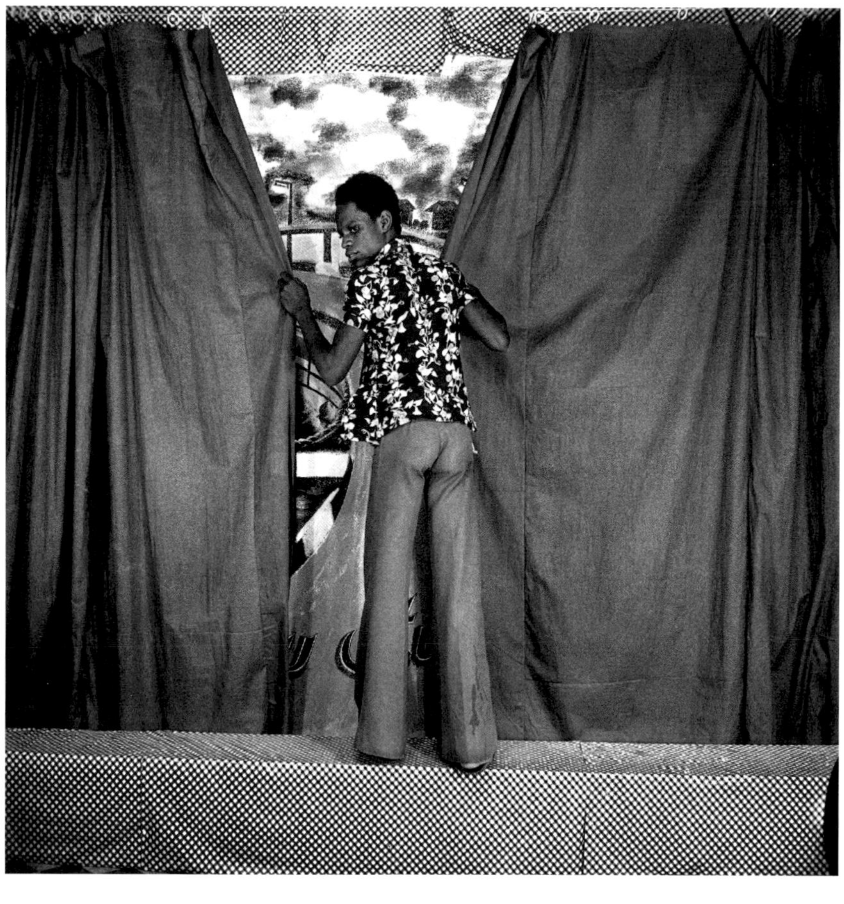

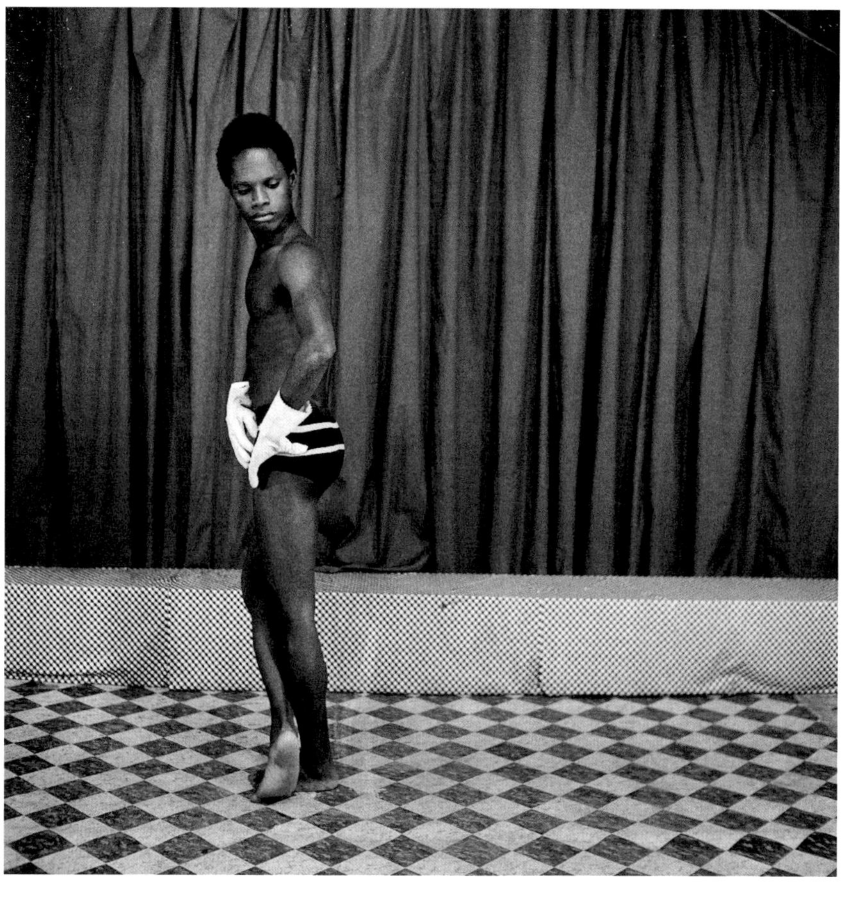

12. *70's Lifestyle* series, 1976–77.

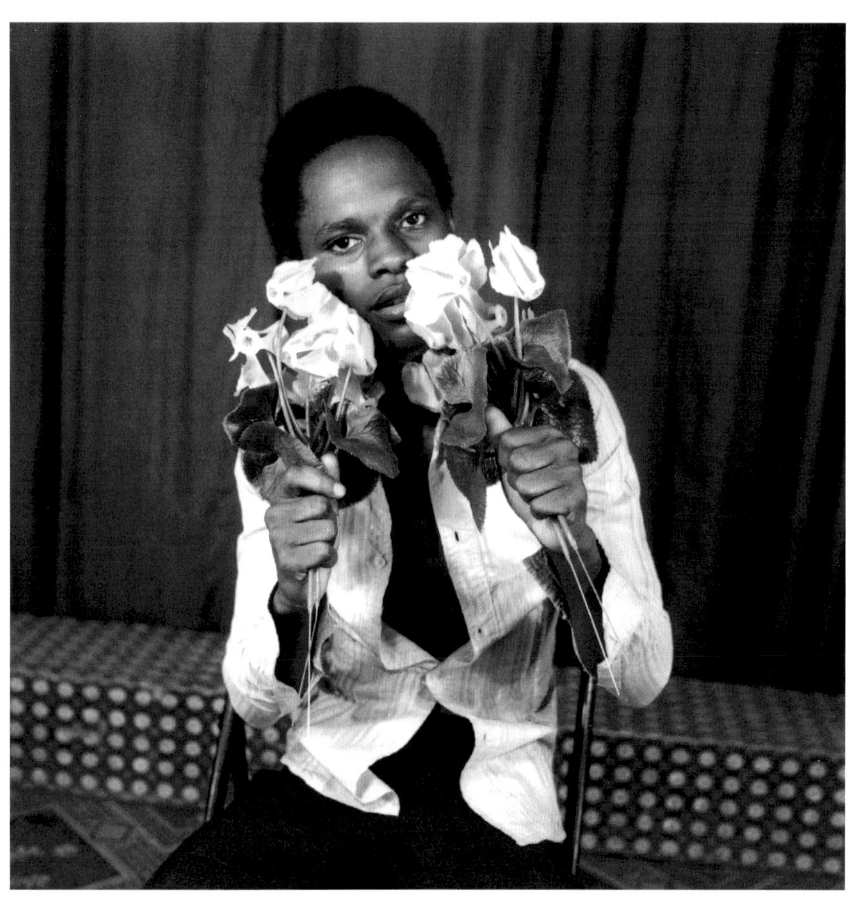

13. *70's Lifestyle* series, 1977.
Samuel Fosso poses in a top handed out to the Central African Republic's Nigerian community for the coronation parade of the self-proclaimed emperor Jean-Bédel Bokassa. The top features the late nationalist leader Barthélemy Boganda, on the left in this photograph, and Jean-Bédel Bokassa, on the right.

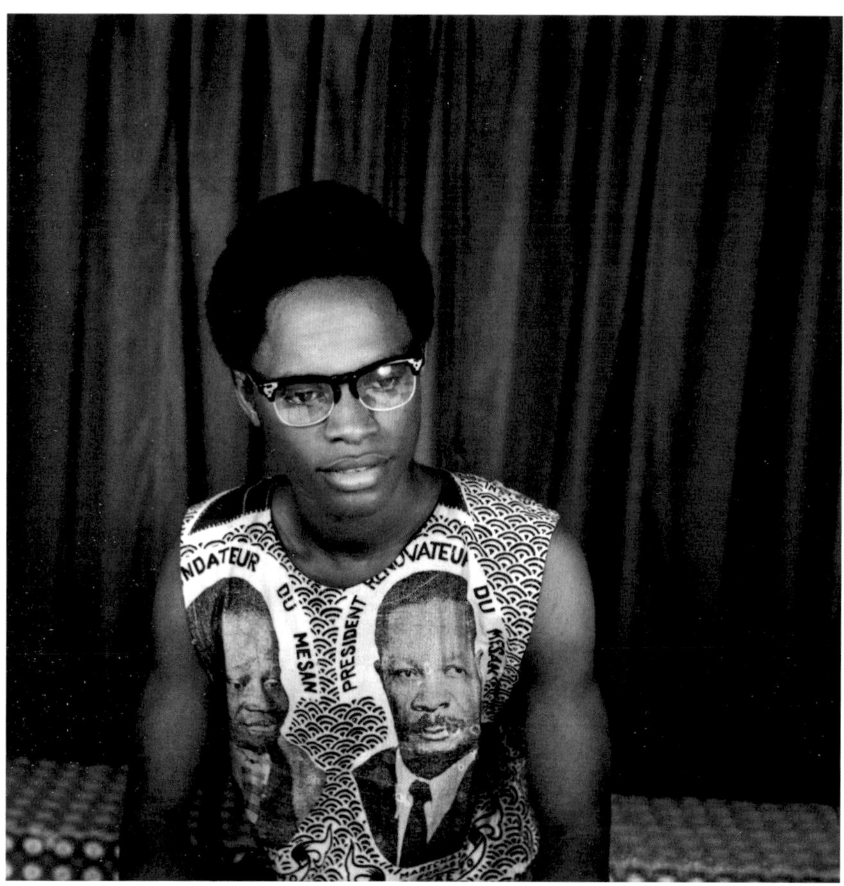
NDATEUR
DU
MESAN
PRESIDENT
RENOVATEUR
DU
MESAN
MARECHAL

14. *70's Lifestyle* series, 1977.

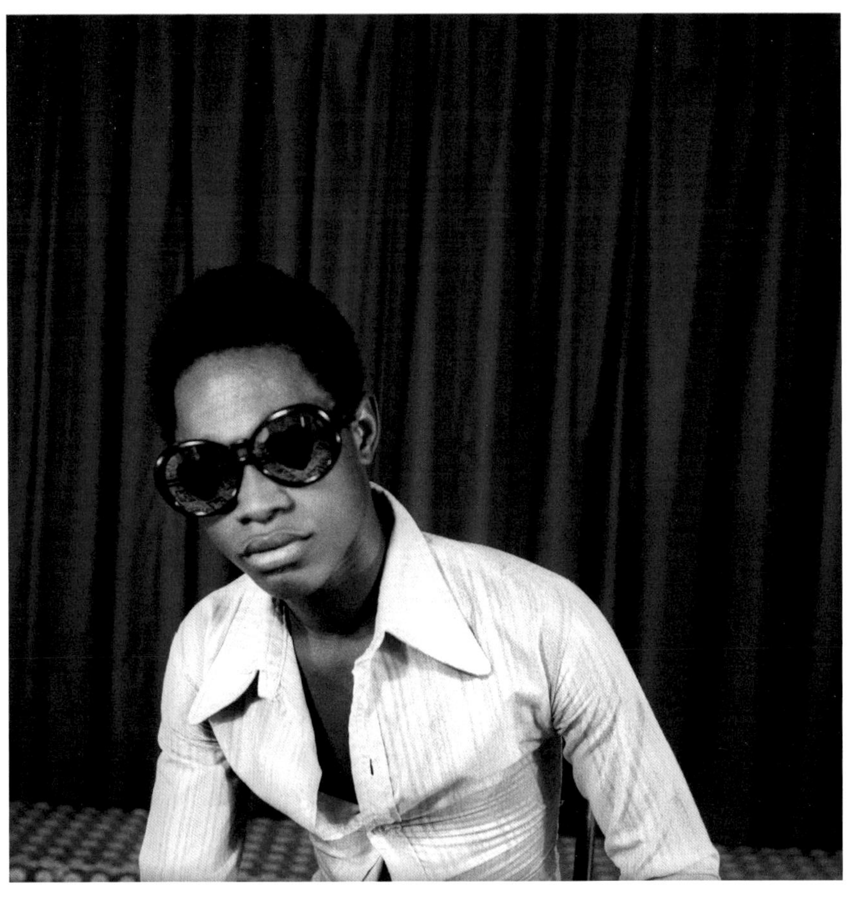

15. *Autoportrait*, 1977. Polaroid print.

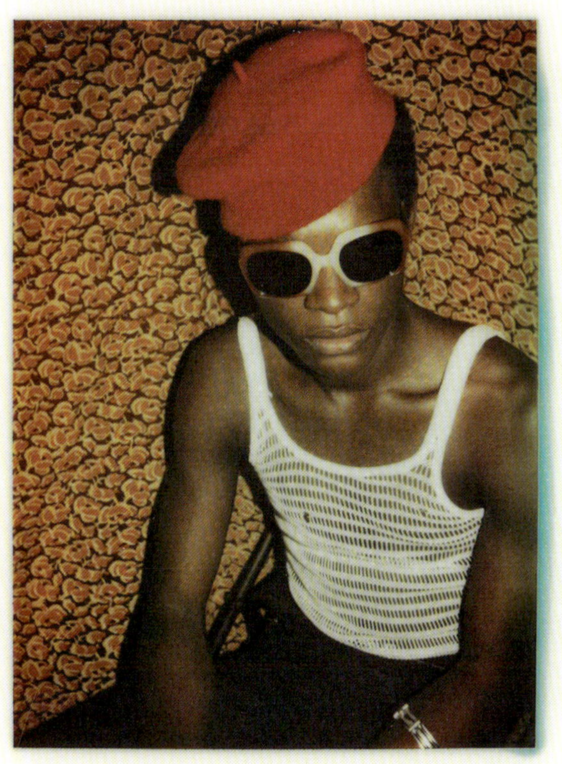

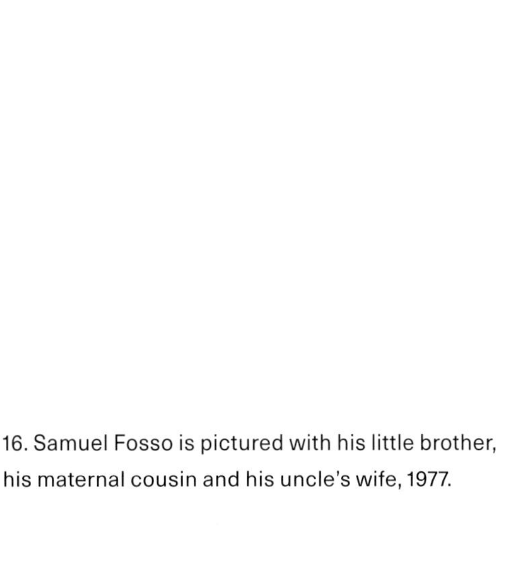

16. Samuel Fosso is pictured with his little brother,
his maternal cousin and his uncle's wife, 1977.

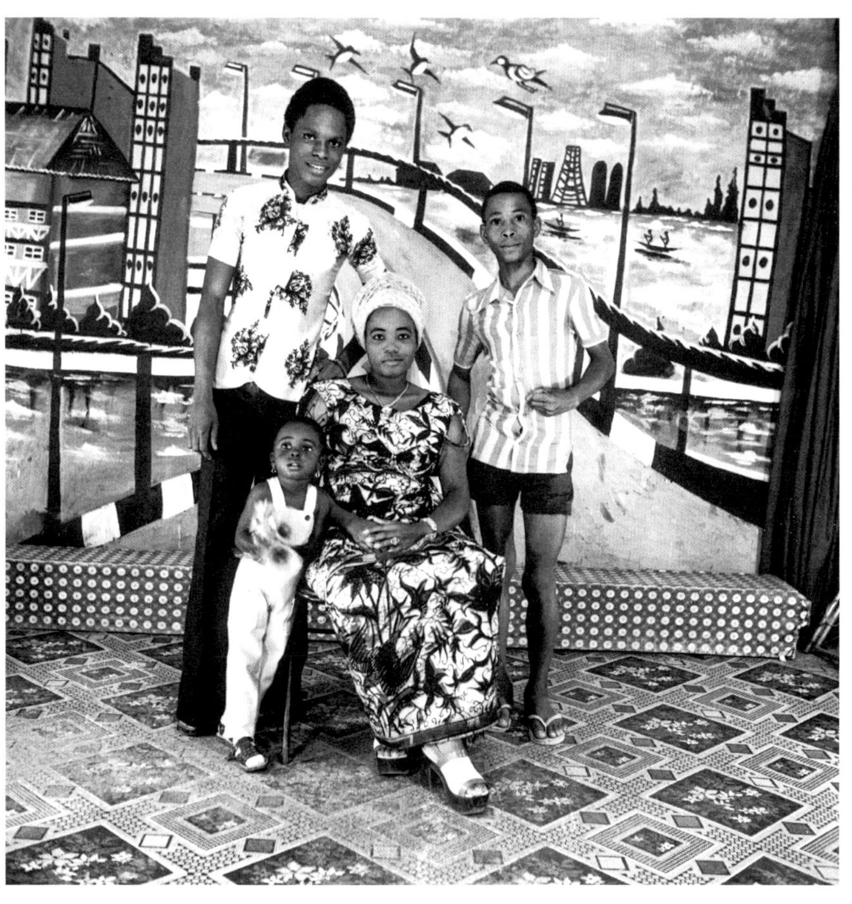

17–18. *70's Lifestyle* series, 1977.

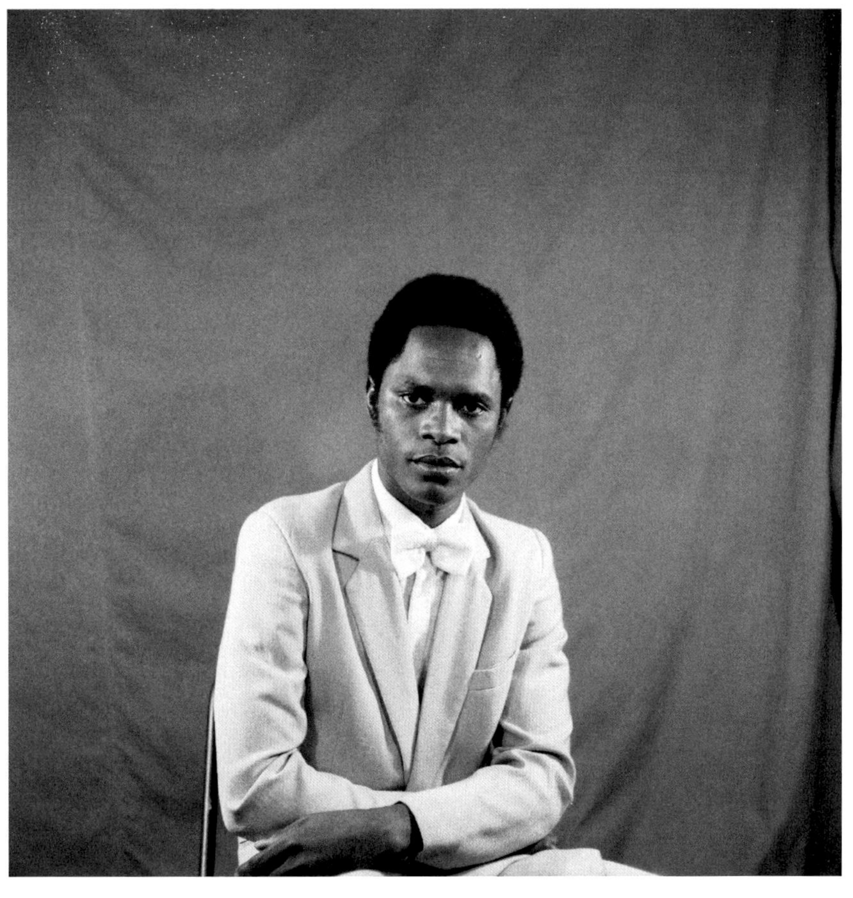

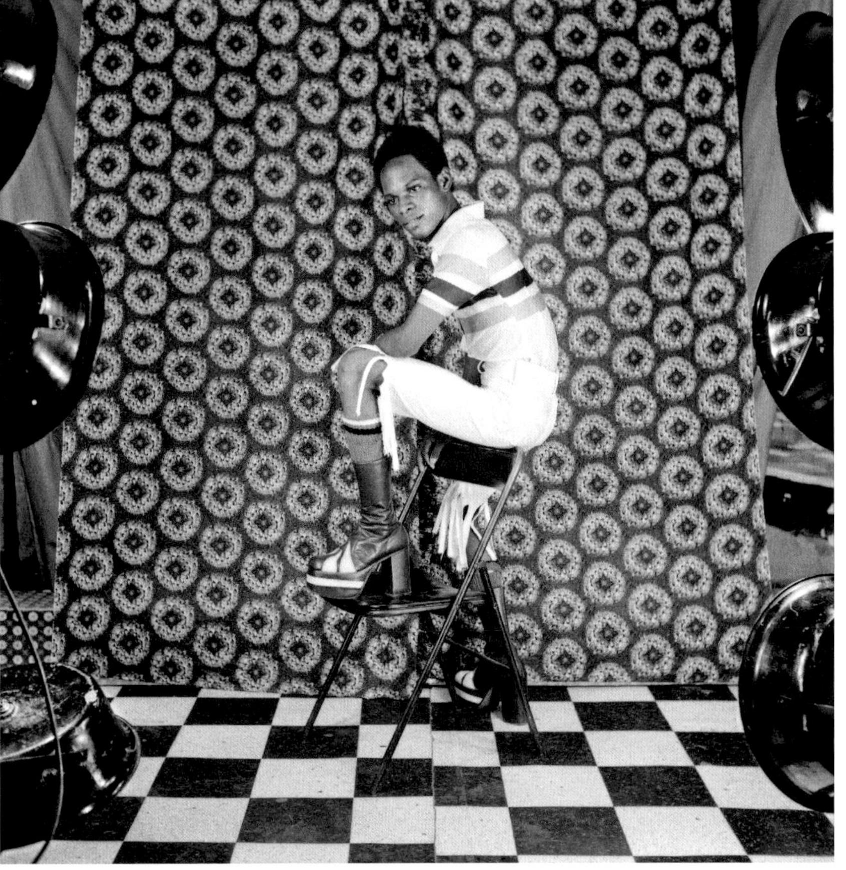

19. *70's Lifestyle* series, 1977.
Samuel Fosso dresses in the style of Cameroonian-
Nigerian musician Prince Nico Mbarga. He wears
a pair of platform boots that were bought in Nigeria
and feature in several photographs.

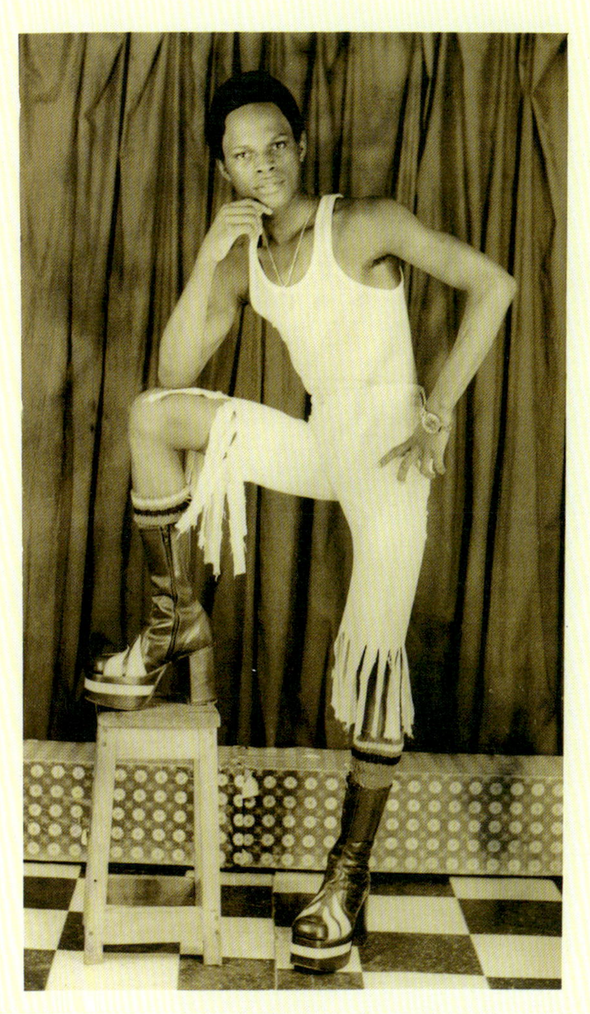

20–25. *70's Lifestyle* series, 1977.

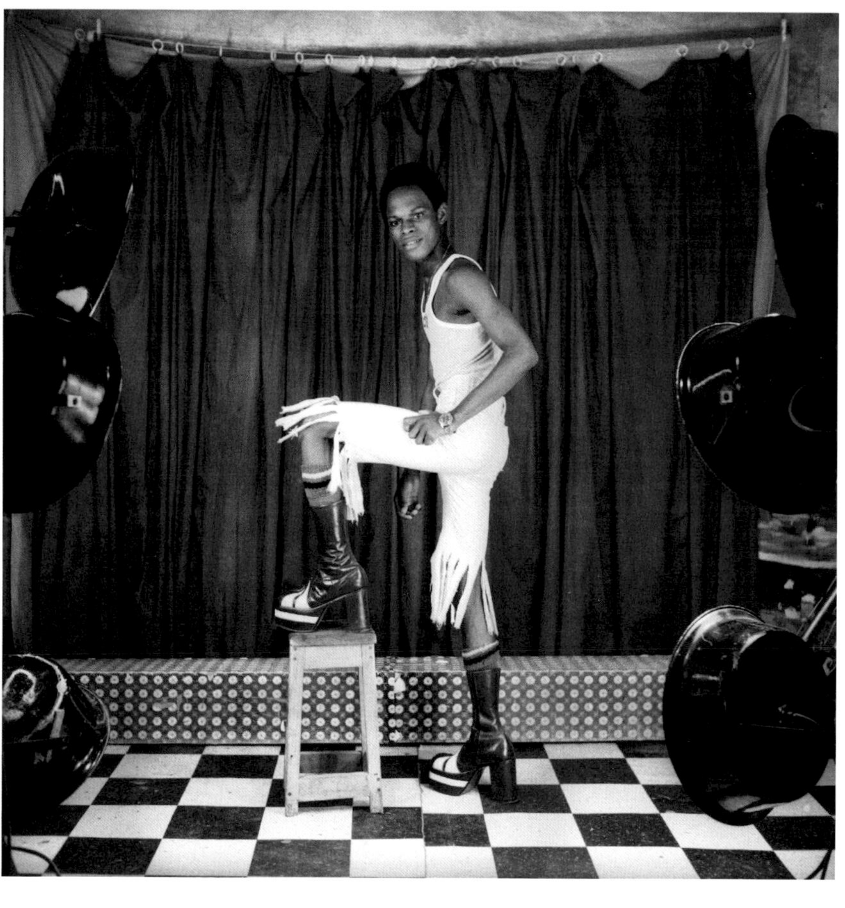

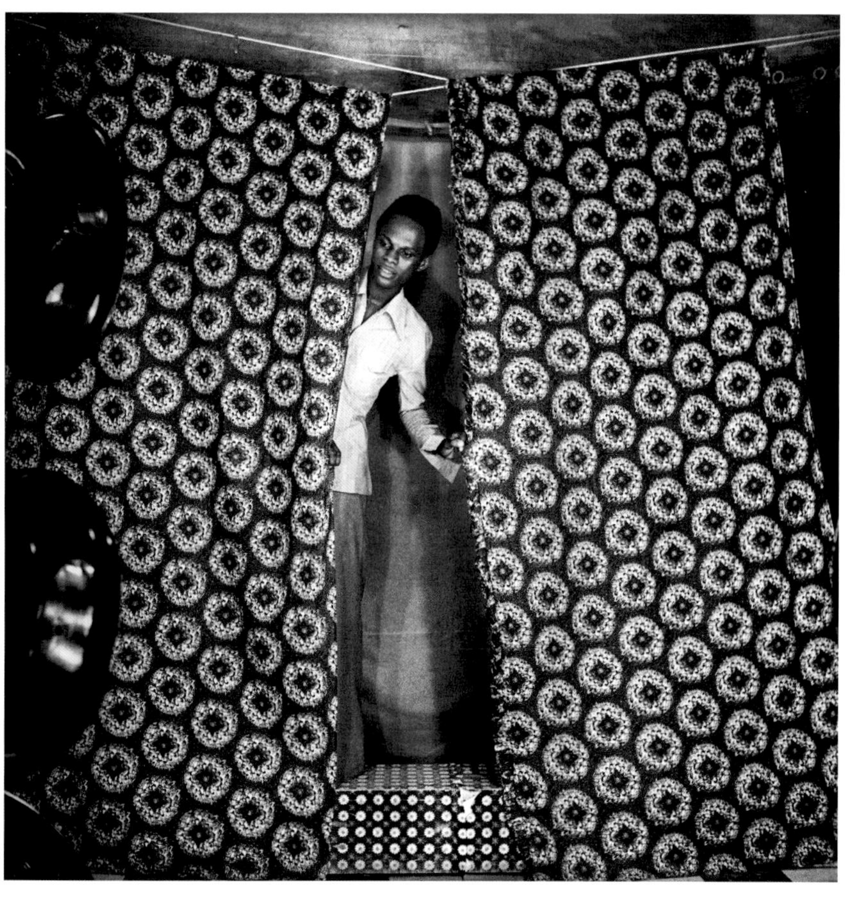

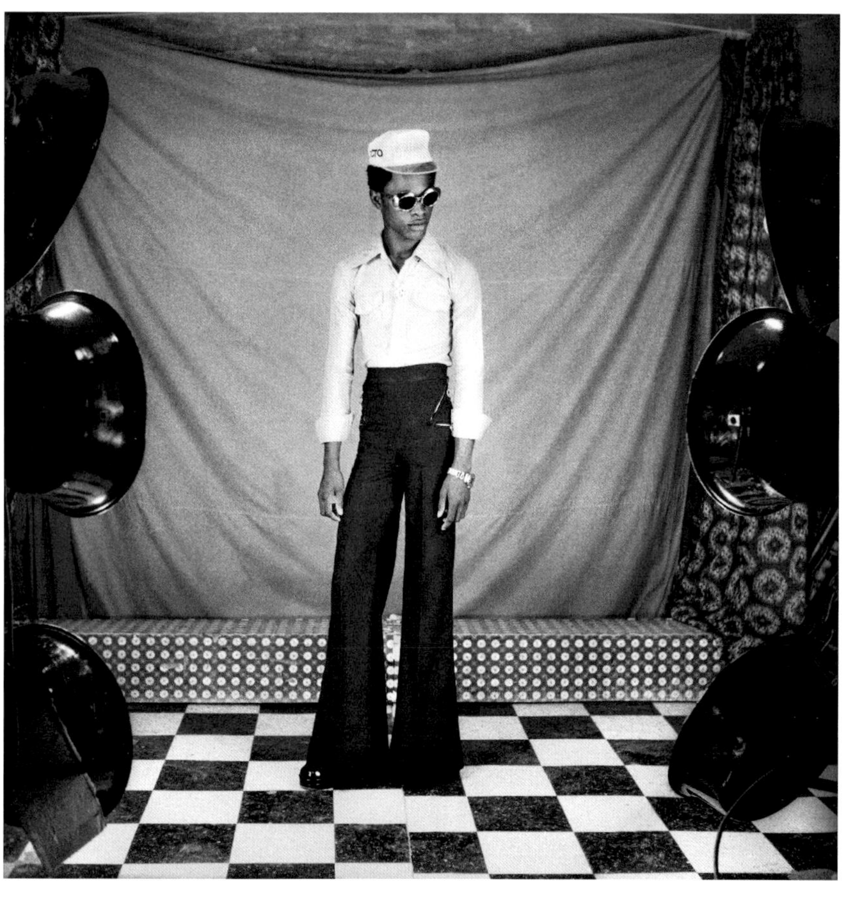

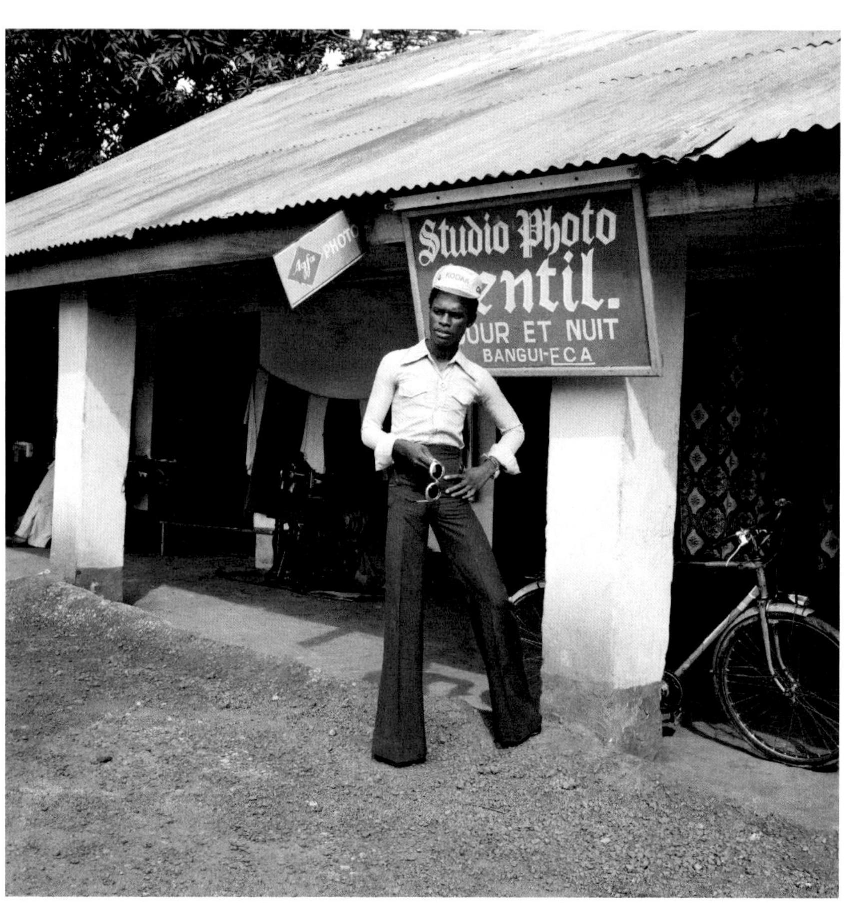

agfa PHOTO
Studio Photo
entil.
OUR ET NUIT
BANGUI-RCA
KODAK

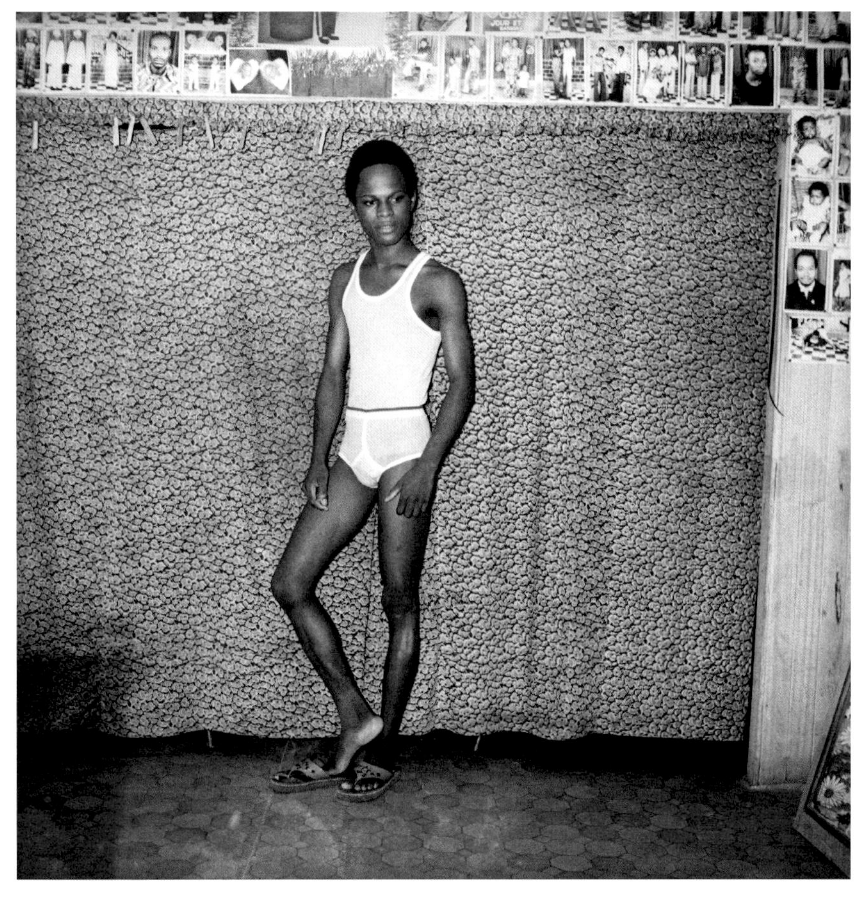

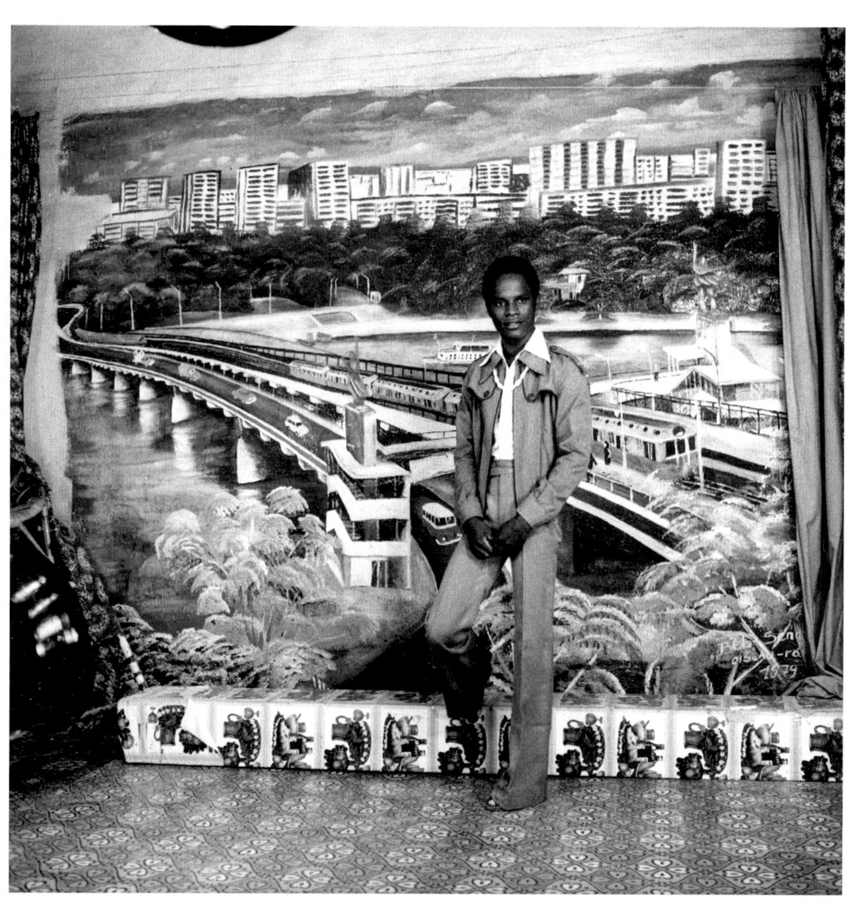

26. *70's Lifestyle* series, 1977–78.

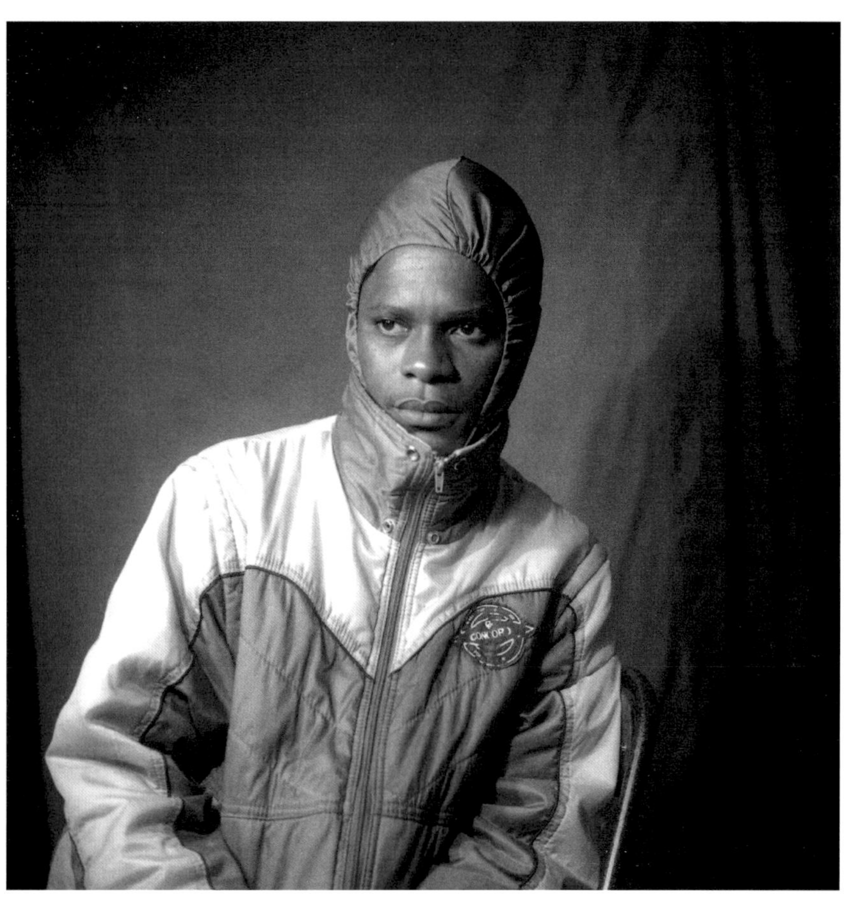

27. Double self-portrait with a friend, 1978. Vintage print.

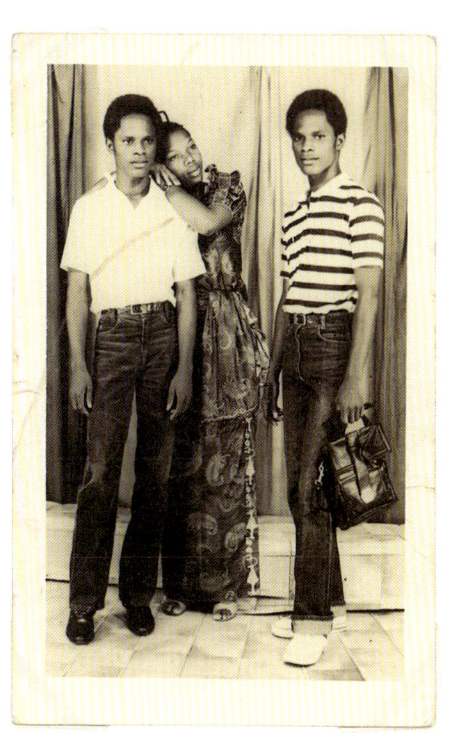

28. Double self-portrait, 1978. Vintage print.

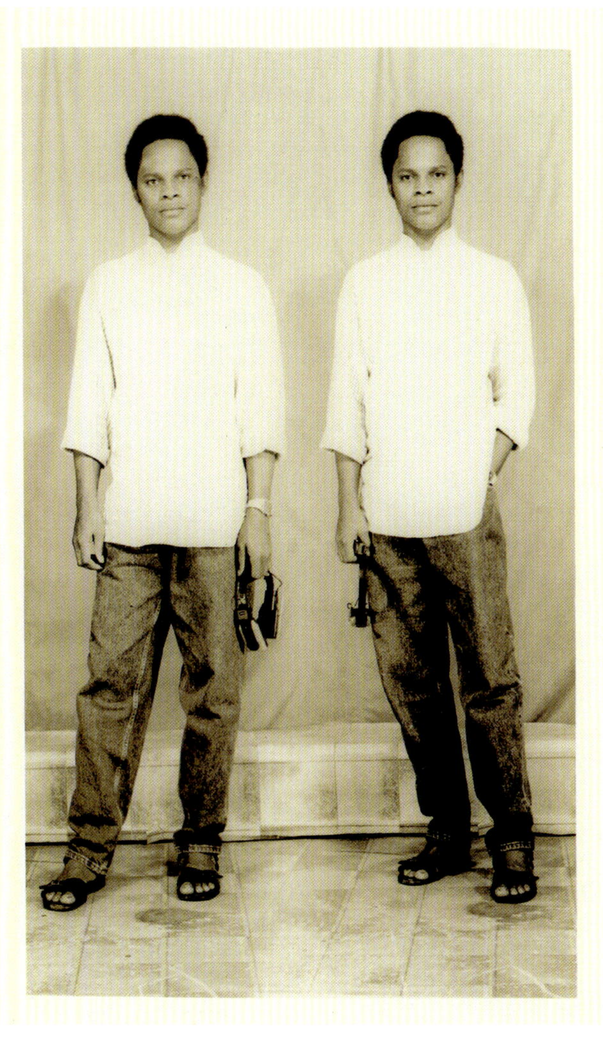

29. 'The Liberated American Woman of the 70s', *Tati* series, 1997.

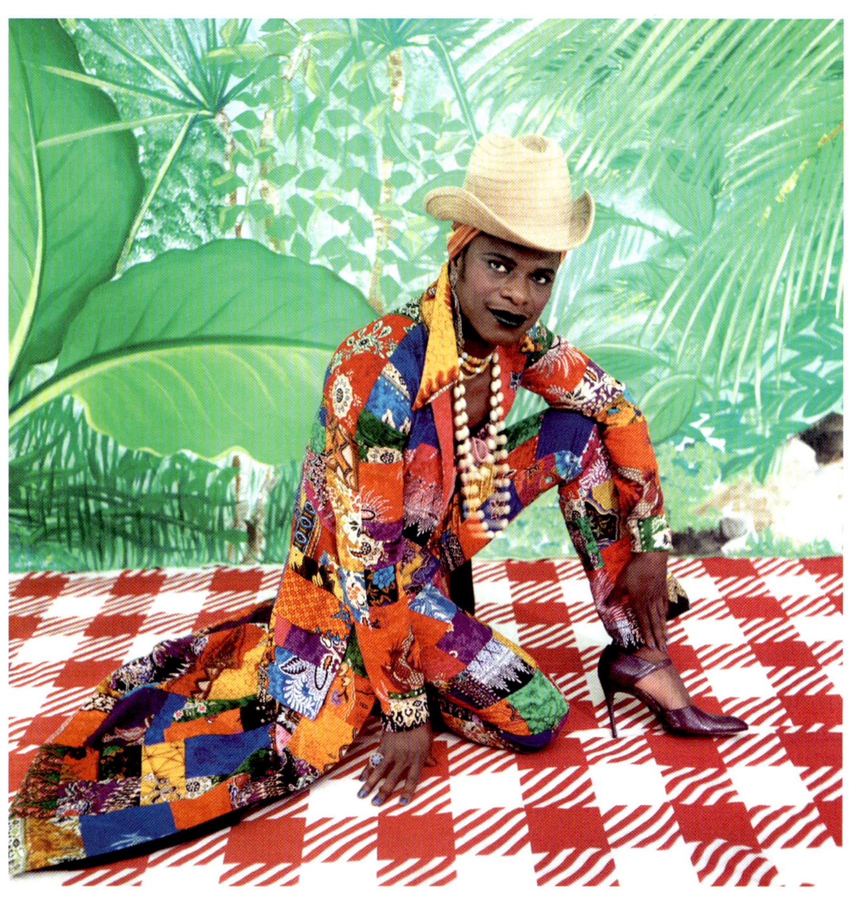

30. 'The Bourgeois Woman', *Tati* series, 1997.

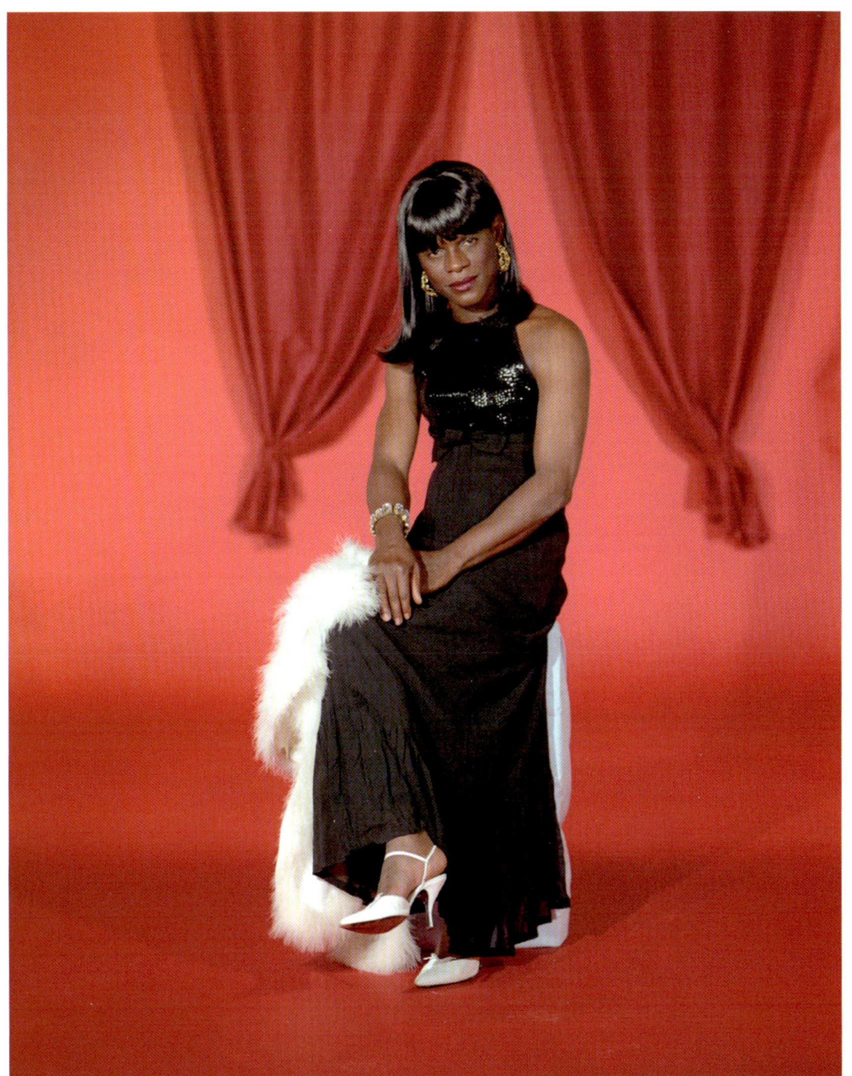

31. 'The Golfer', *Tati* series, 1997.

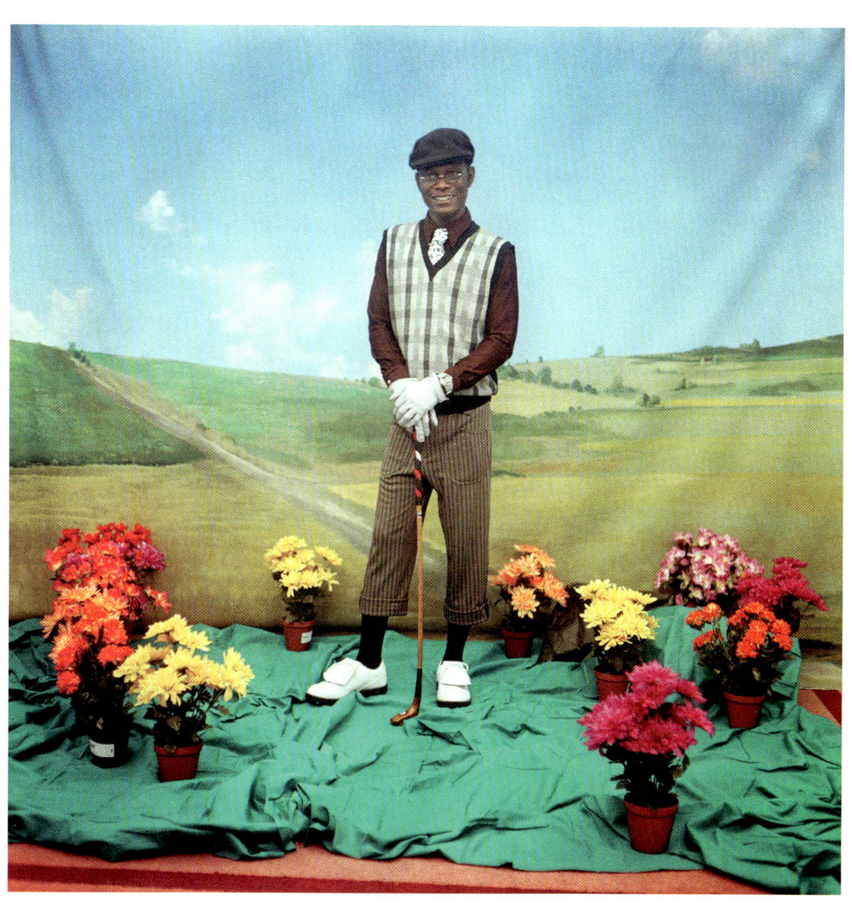

32. 'The Lifeguard', *Tati* series, 1997.

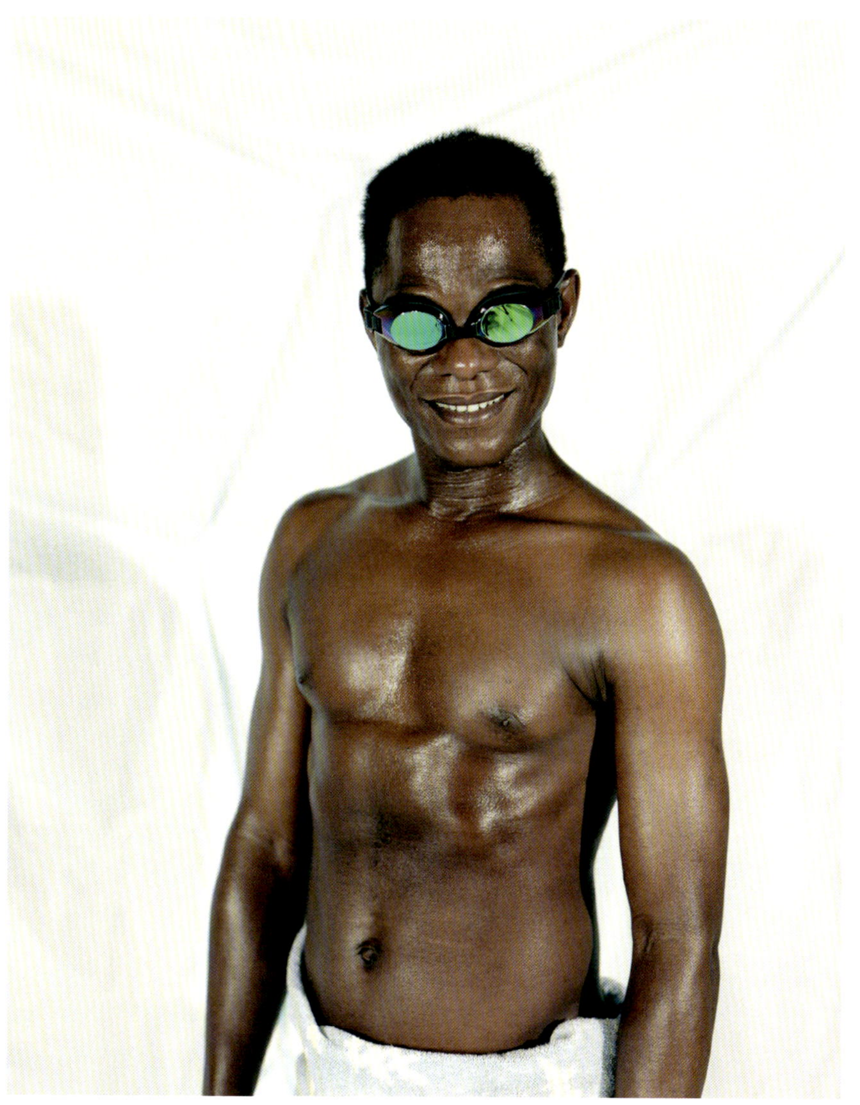

33. 'The Chief (the One who Sold Africa to the Colonists)', *Tati* series, 1997.

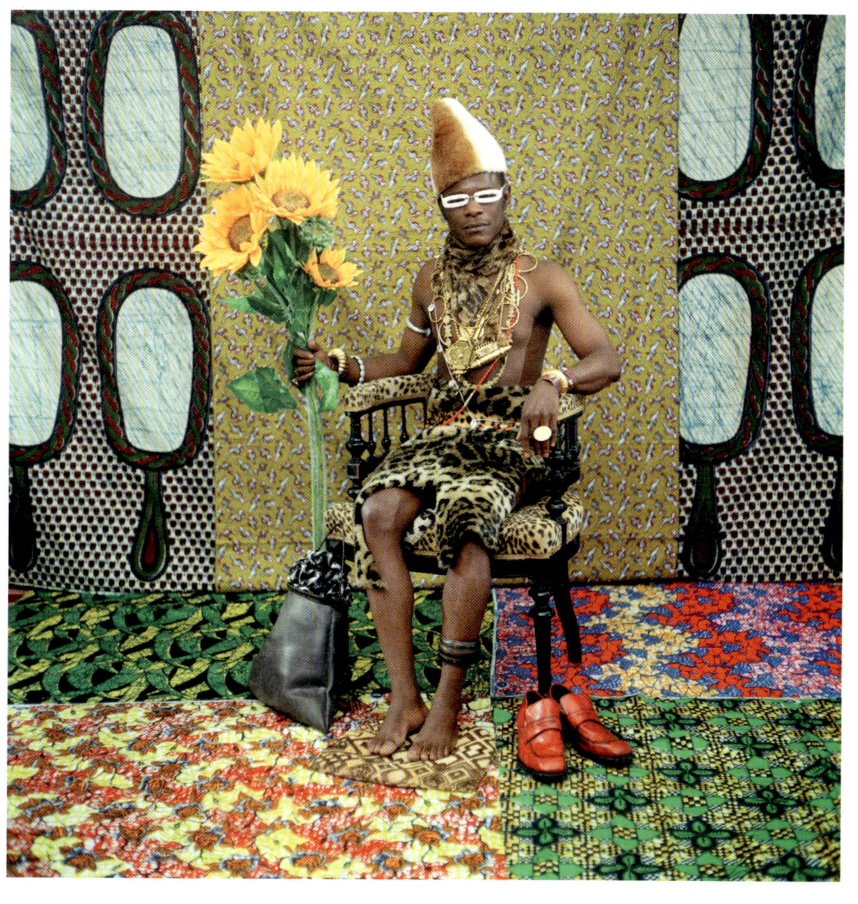

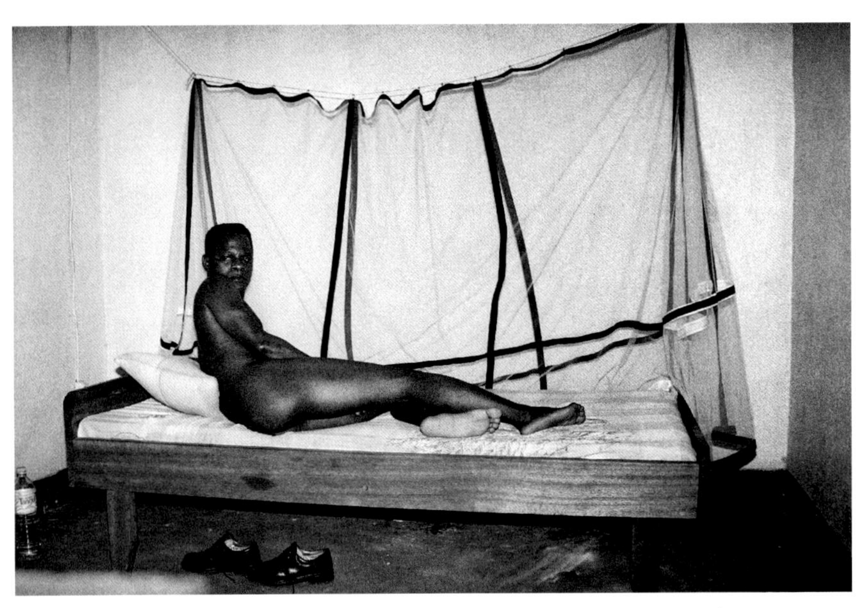

34–39. *Mémoire d'un ami* series, 2000.

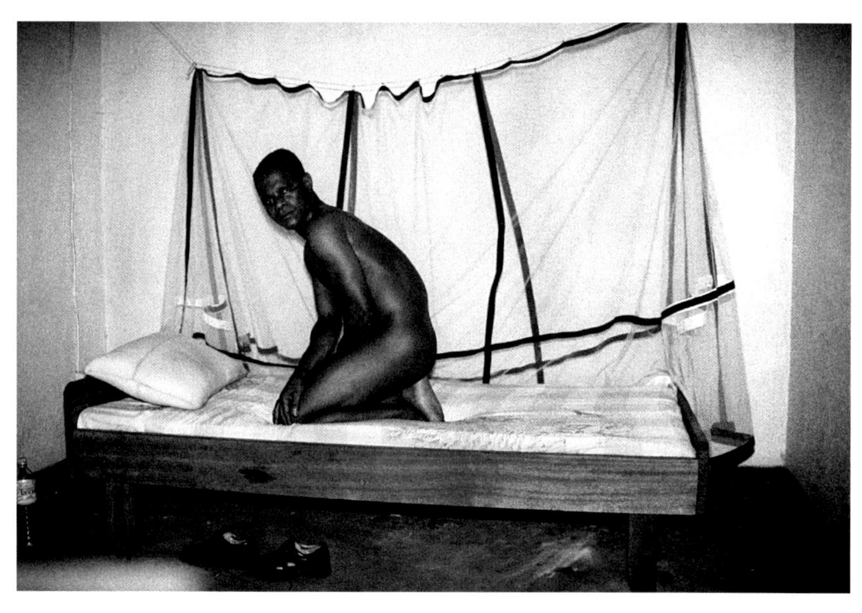

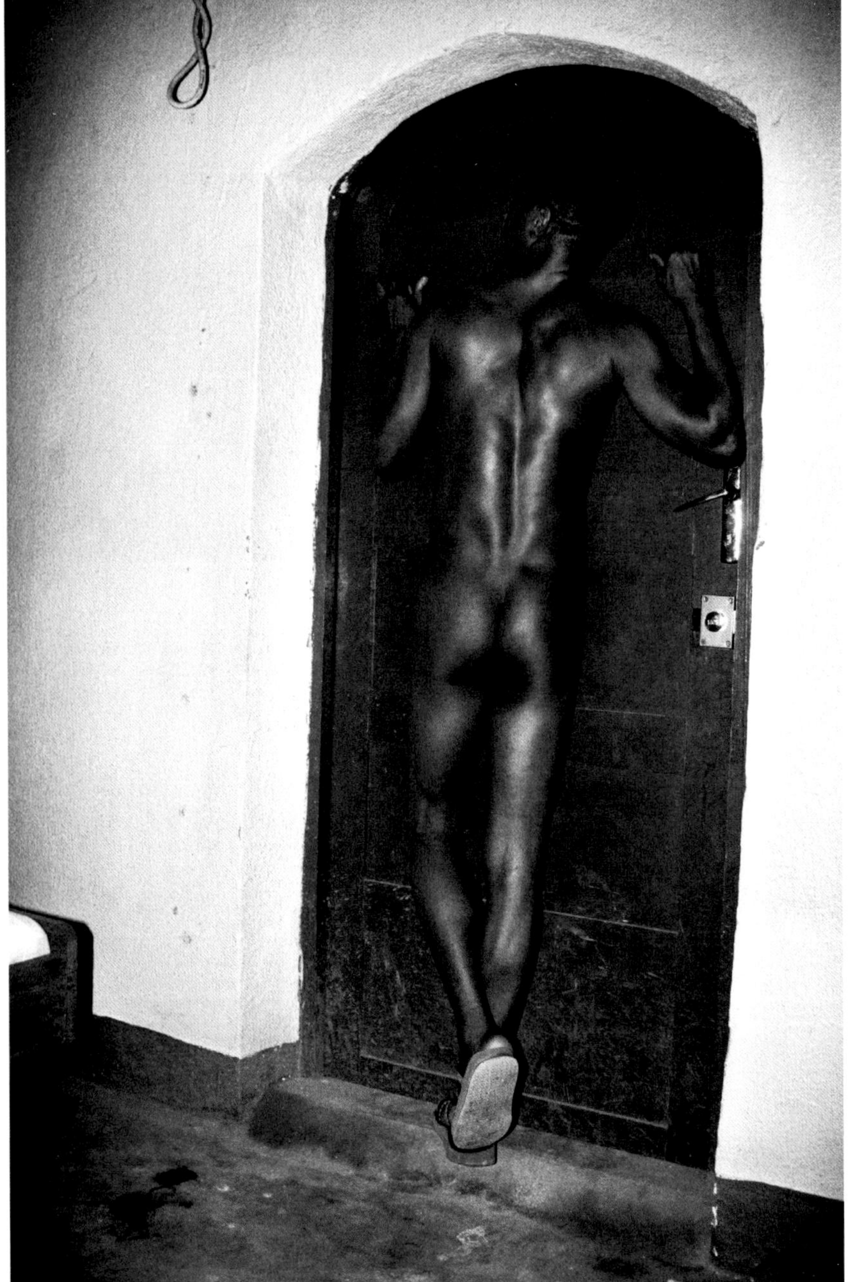

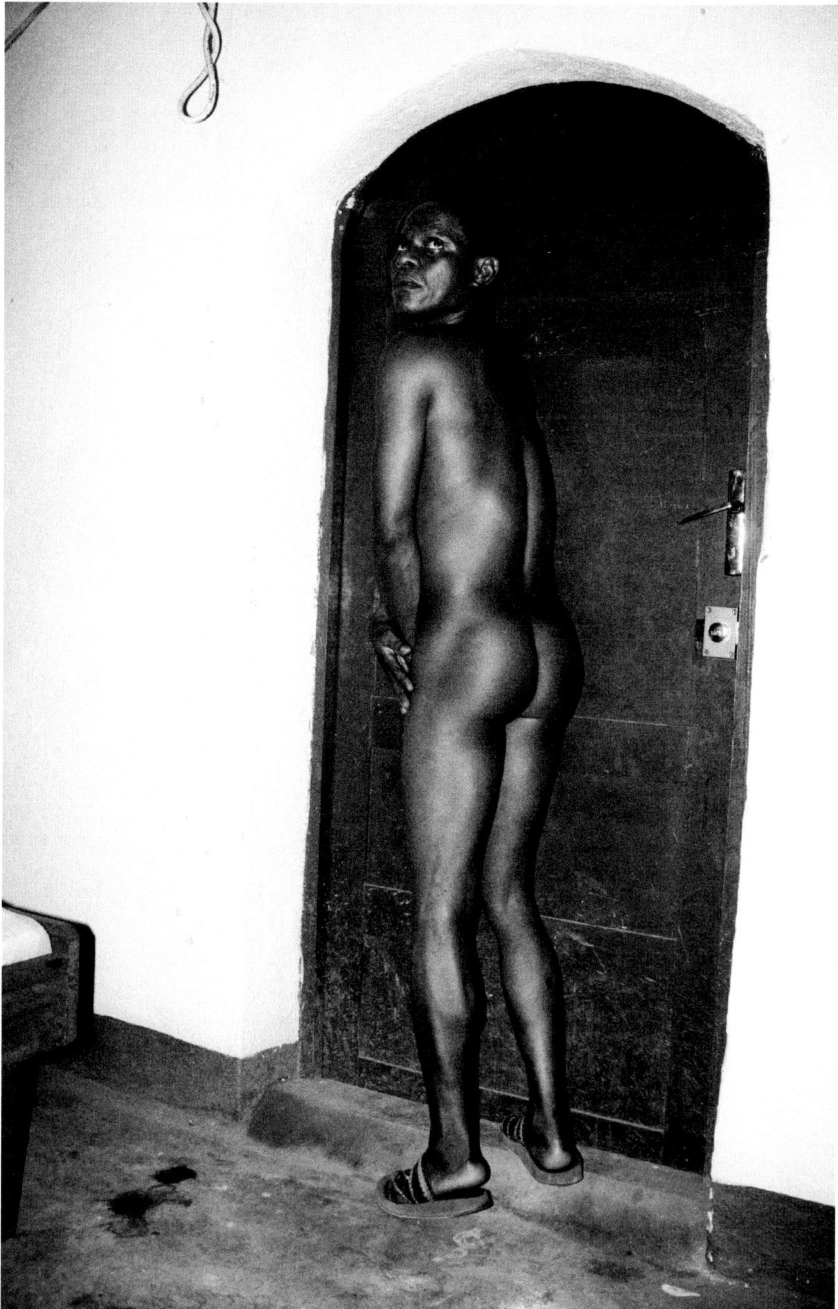

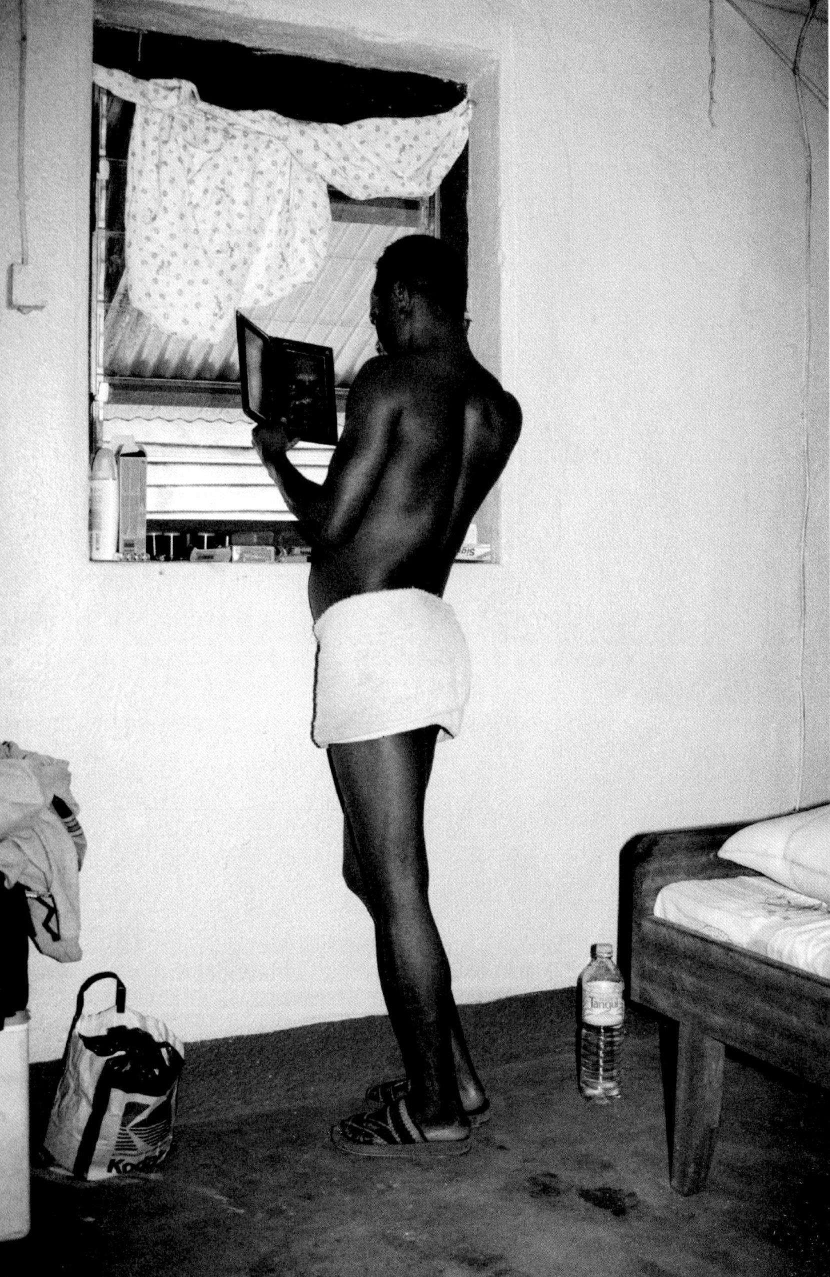

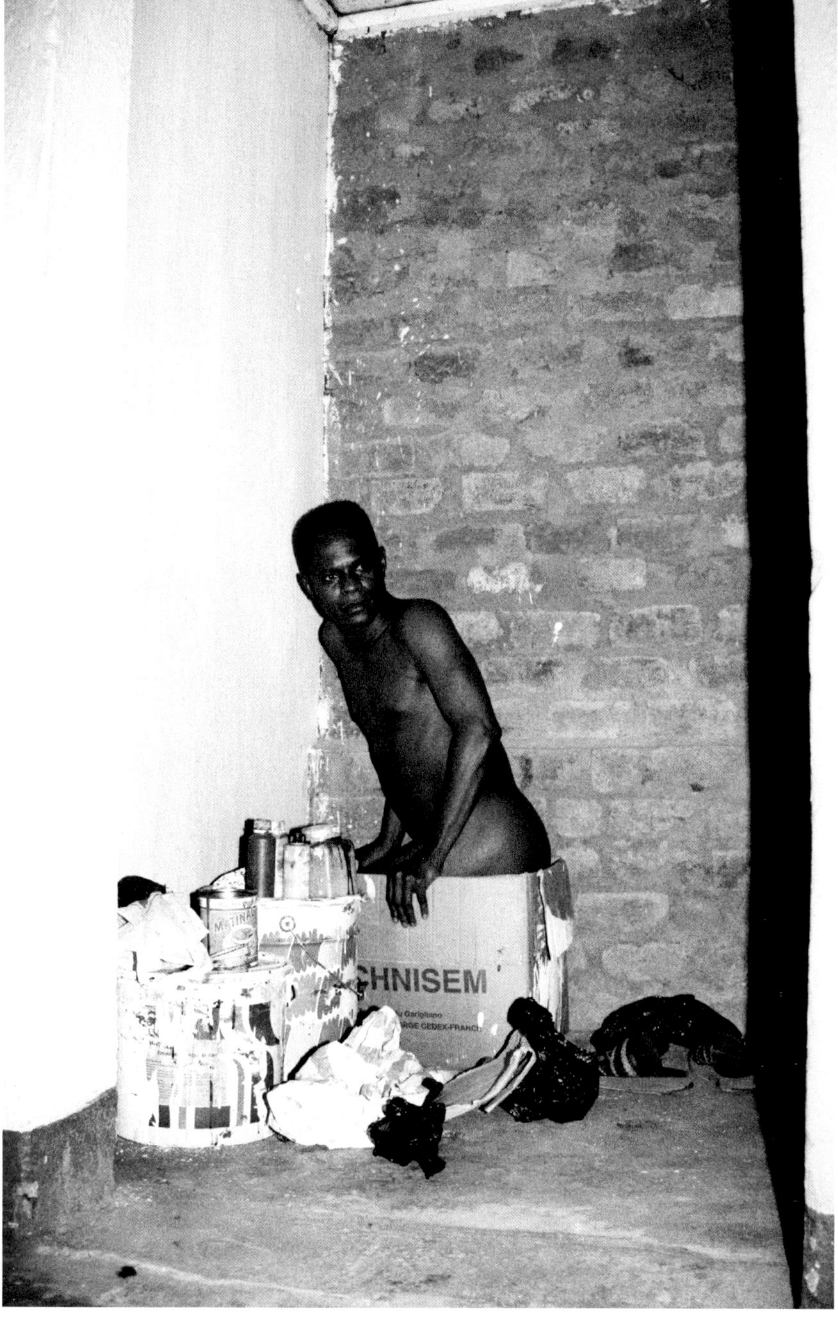
CHNISEM
du Garigliano
RGE CEDEX-FRANC
MATINA

40–45. *Le Rêve de mon grand-père* series, 2003.

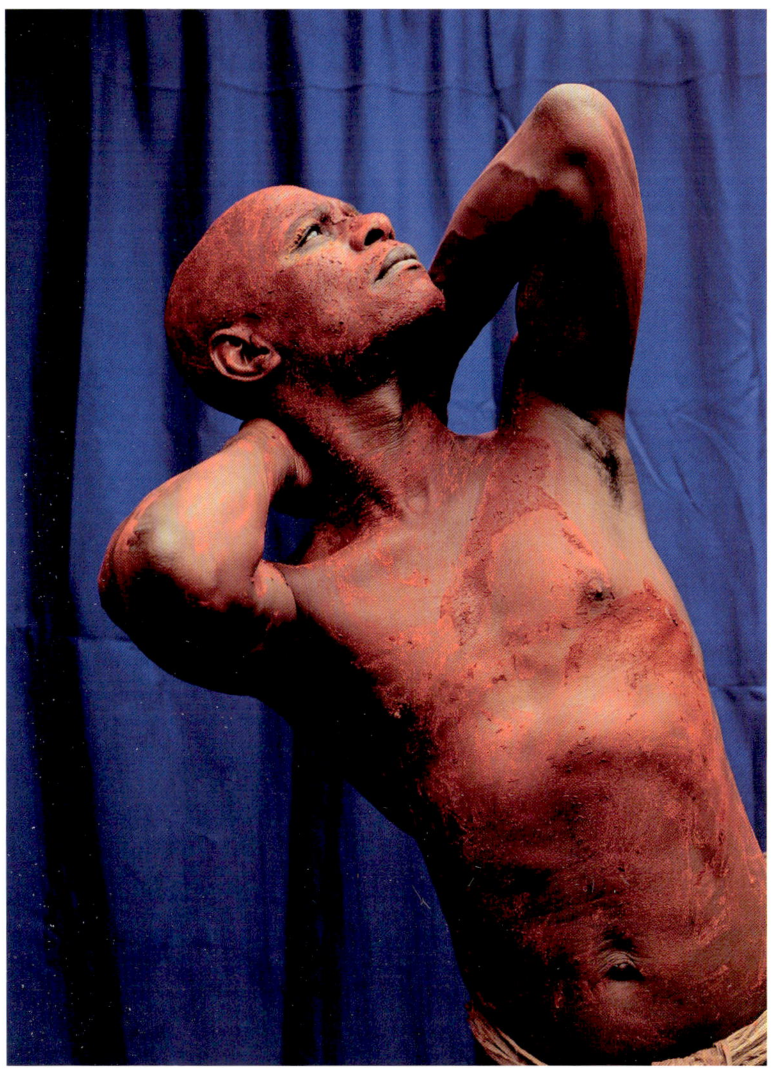

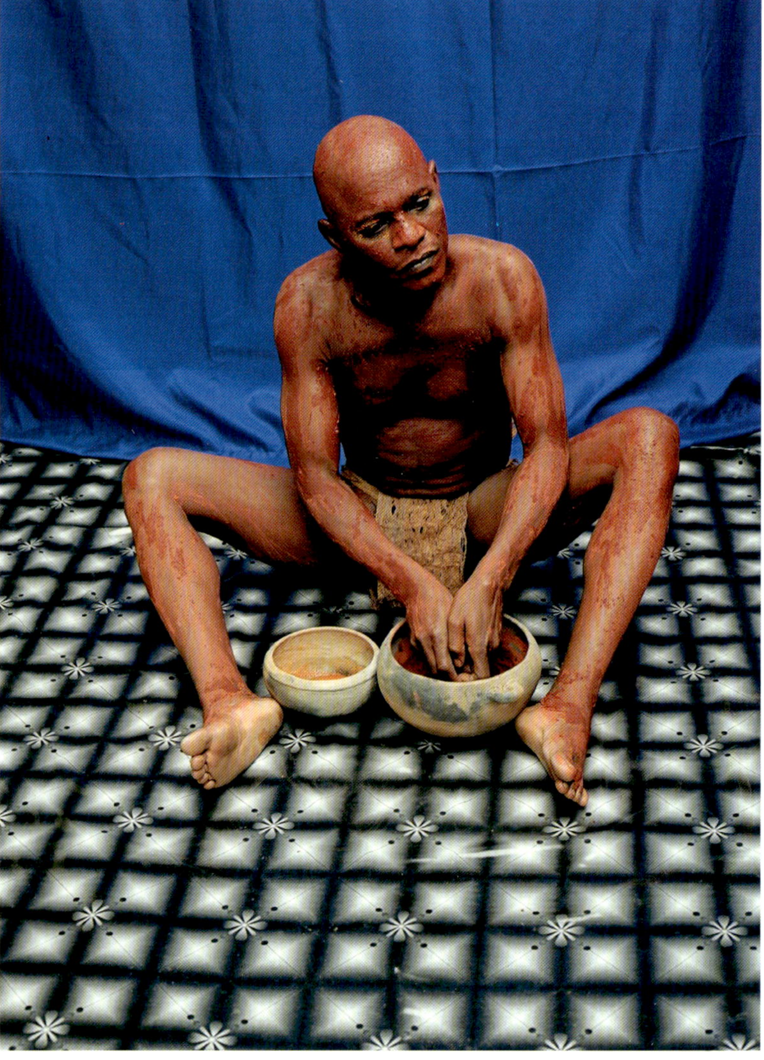

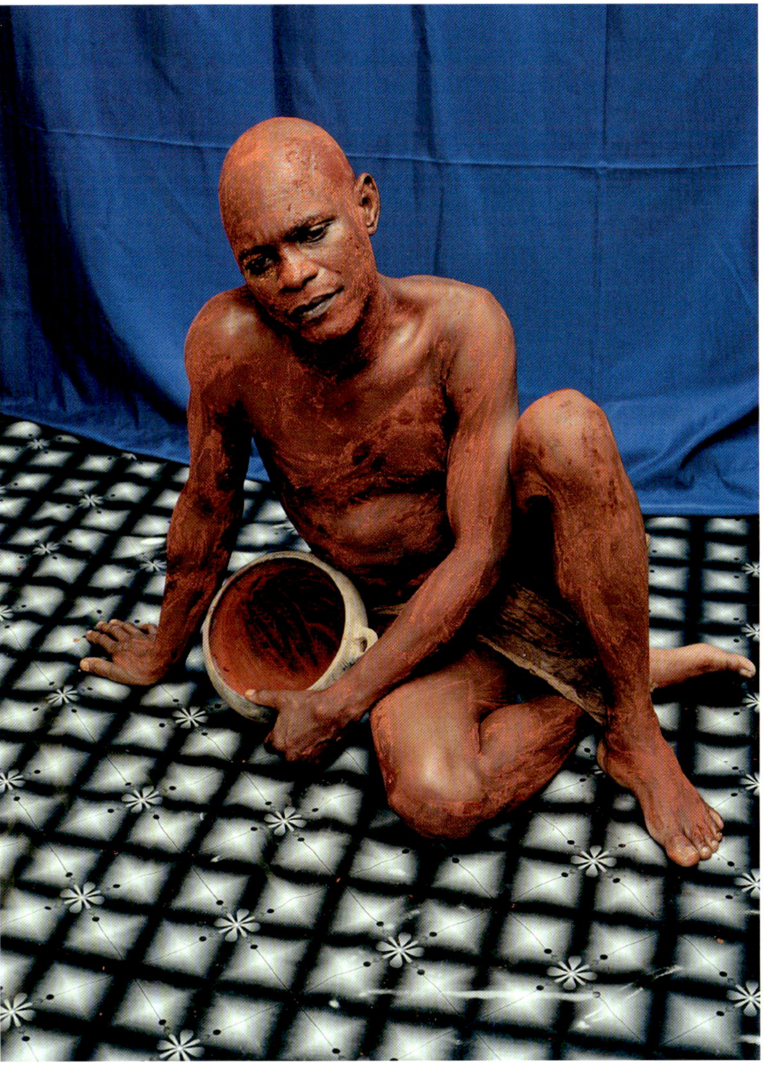

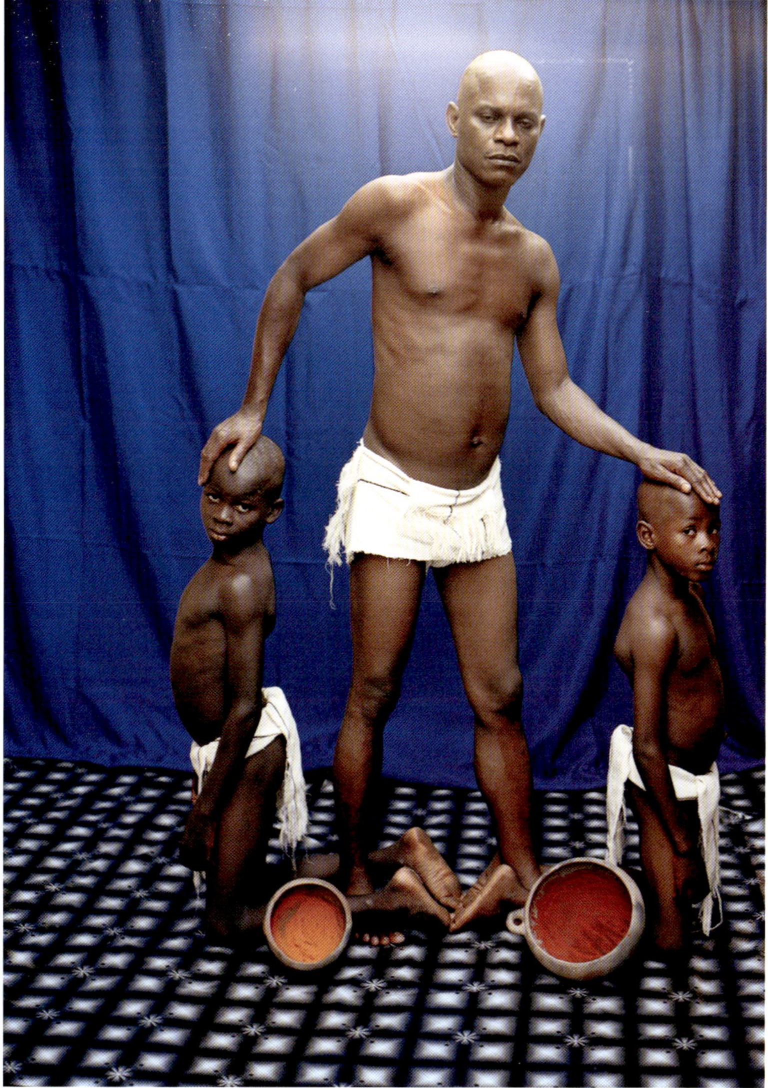

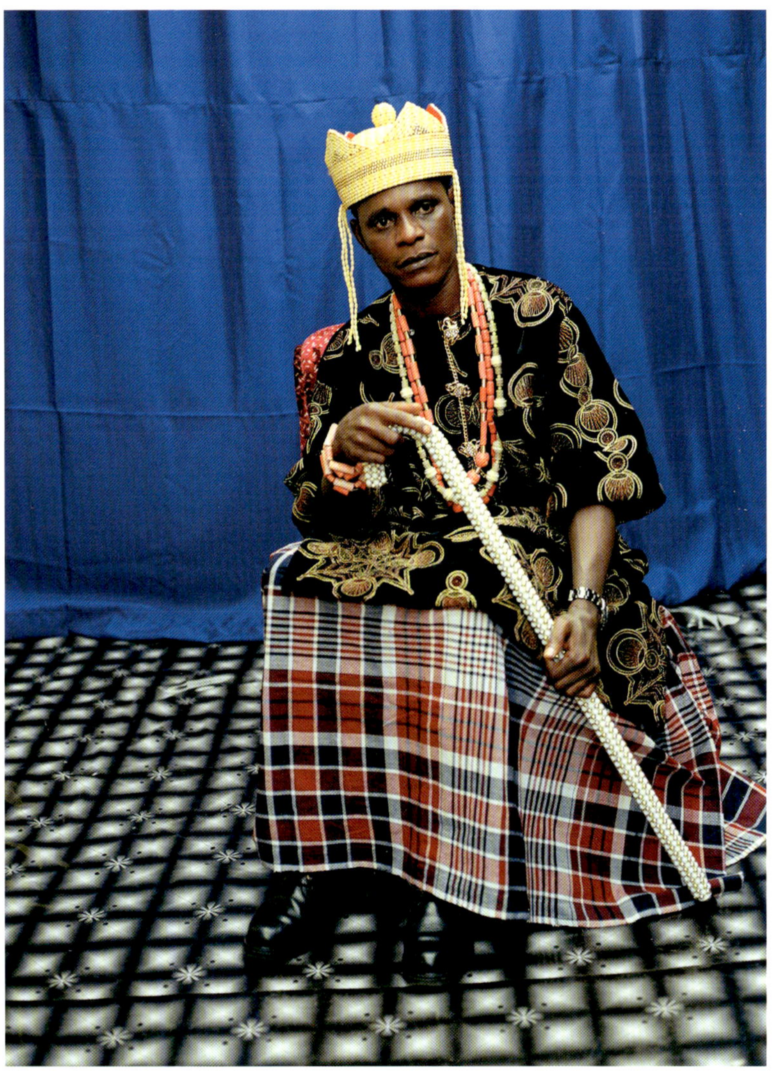

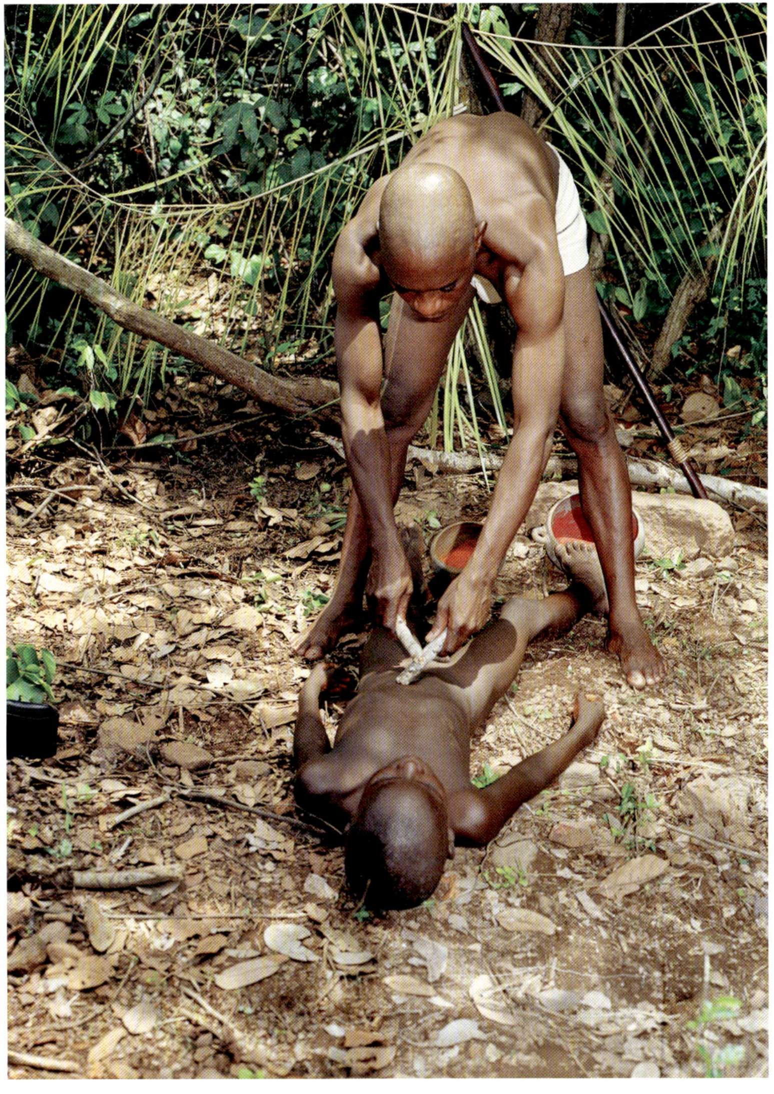

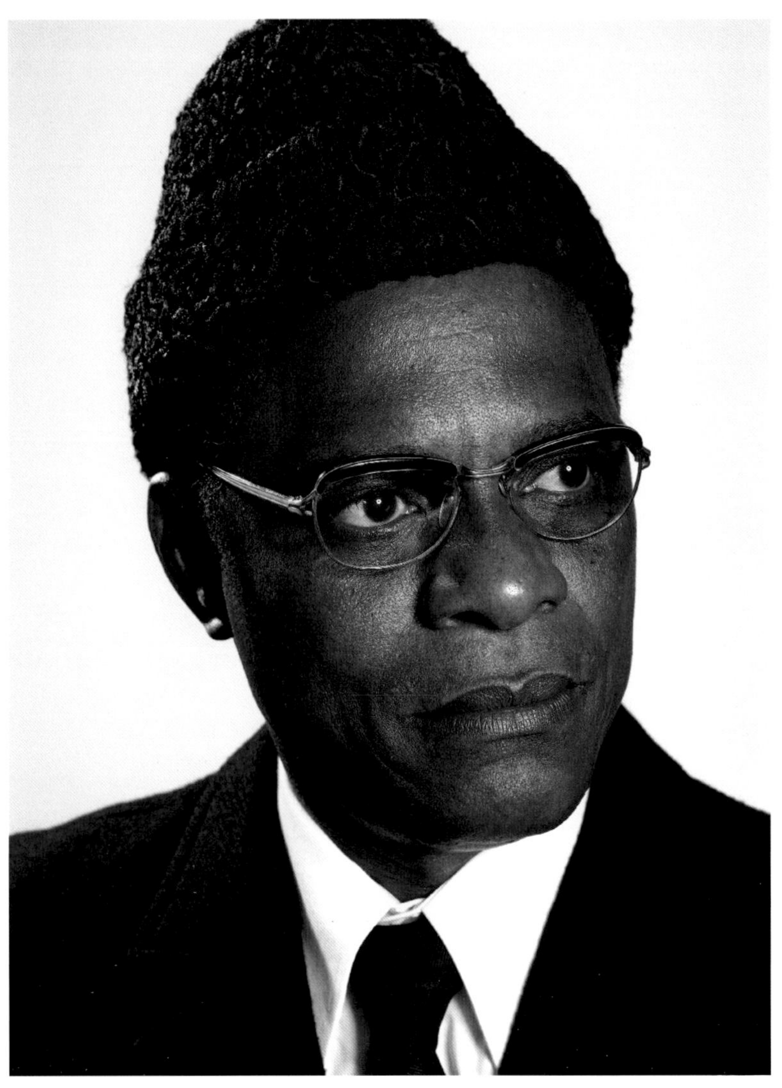

46–55. *African Spirits* series, 2008.

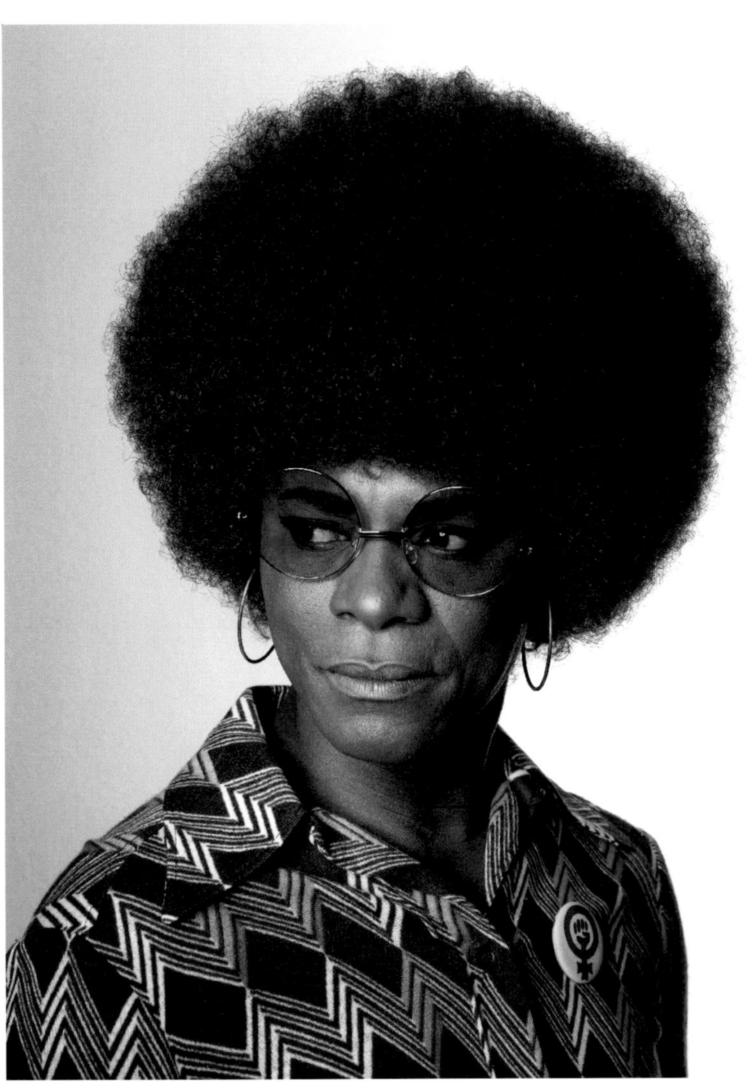

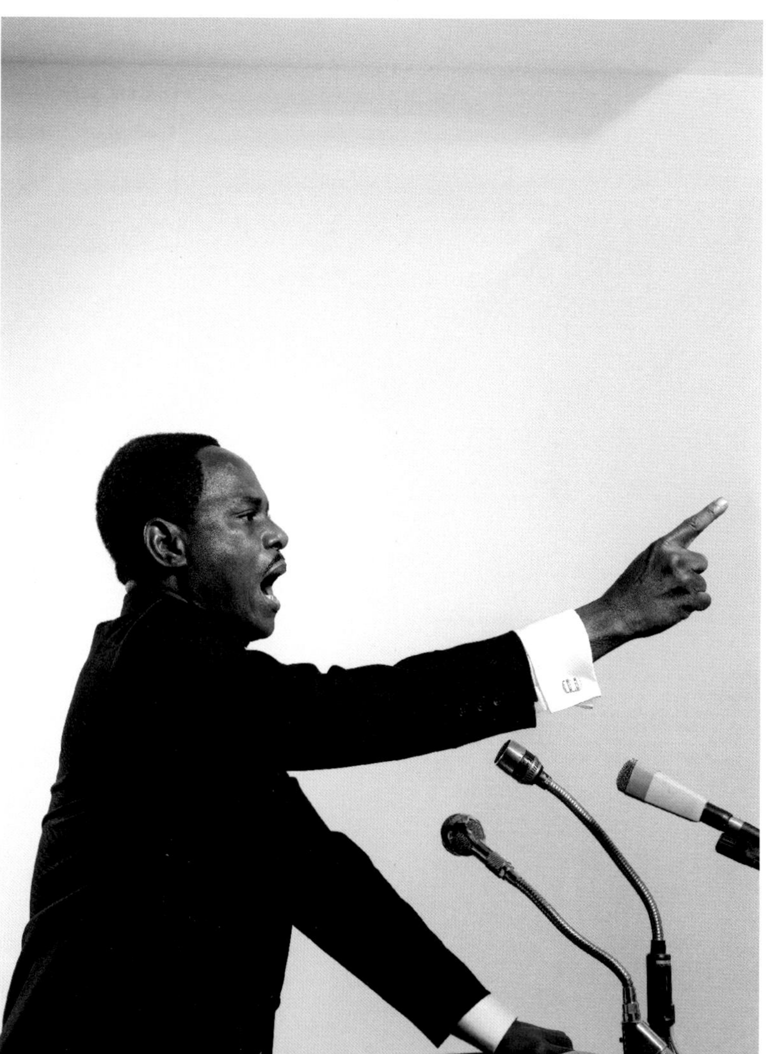

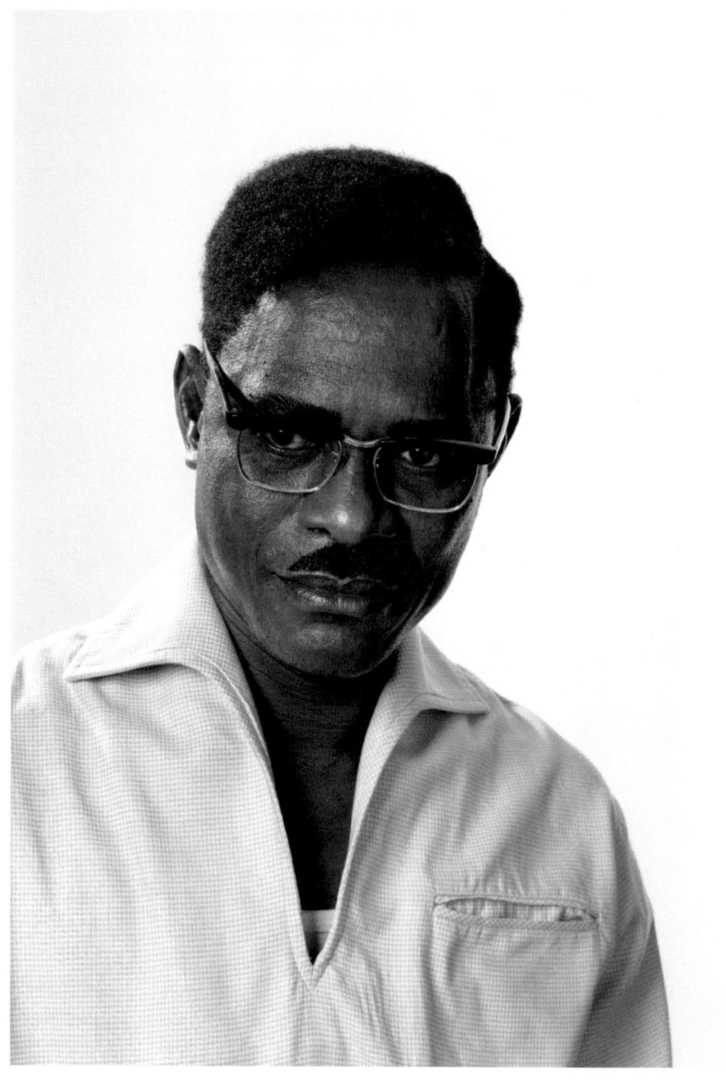

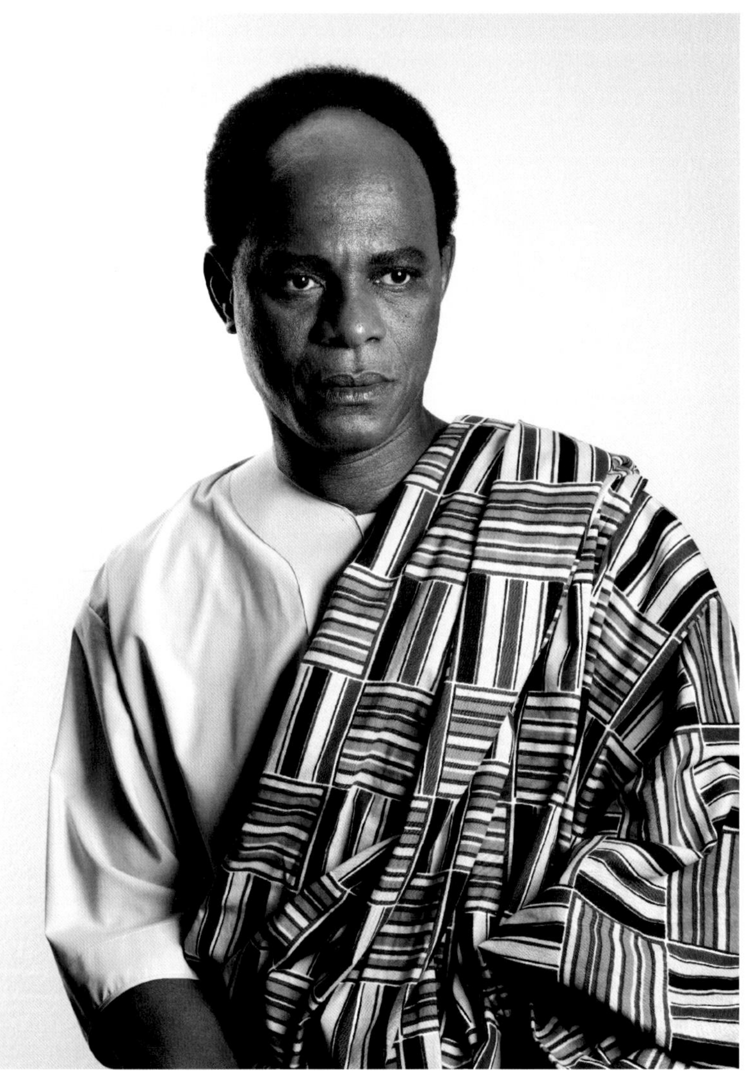

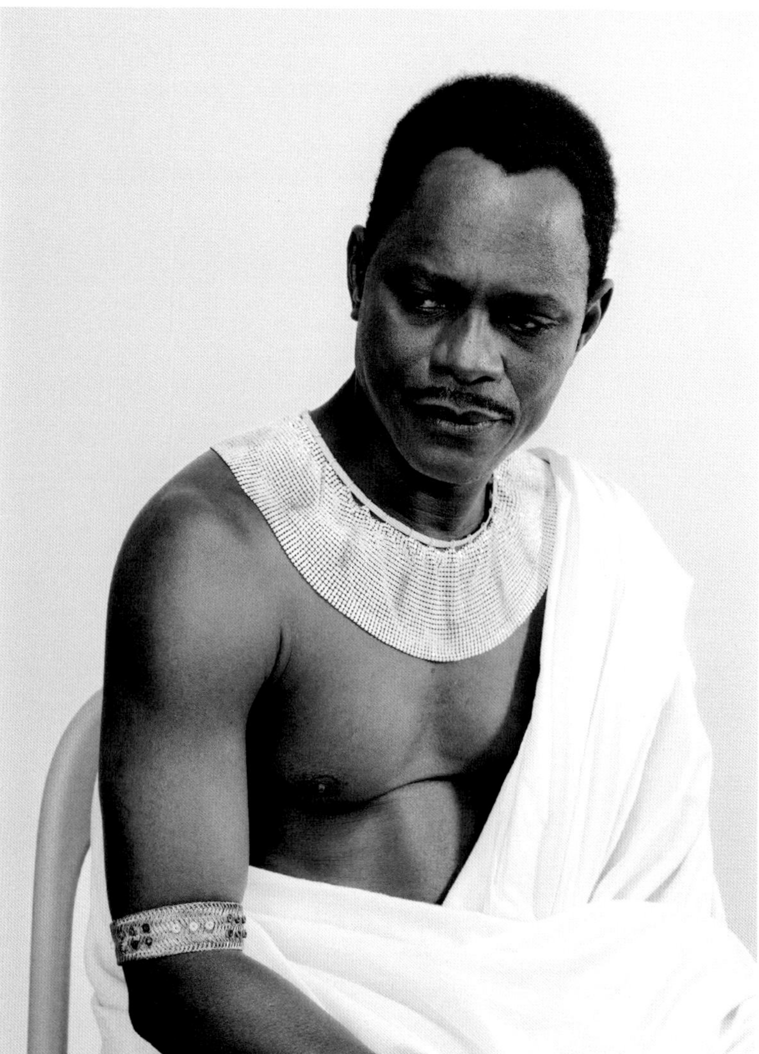

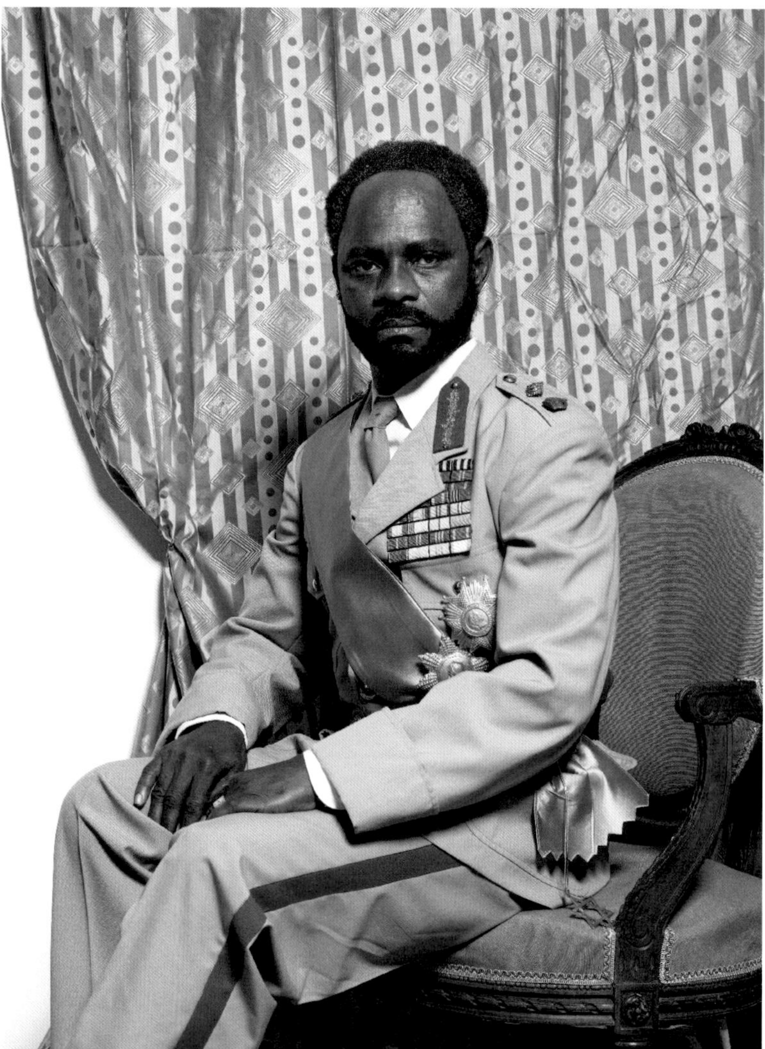

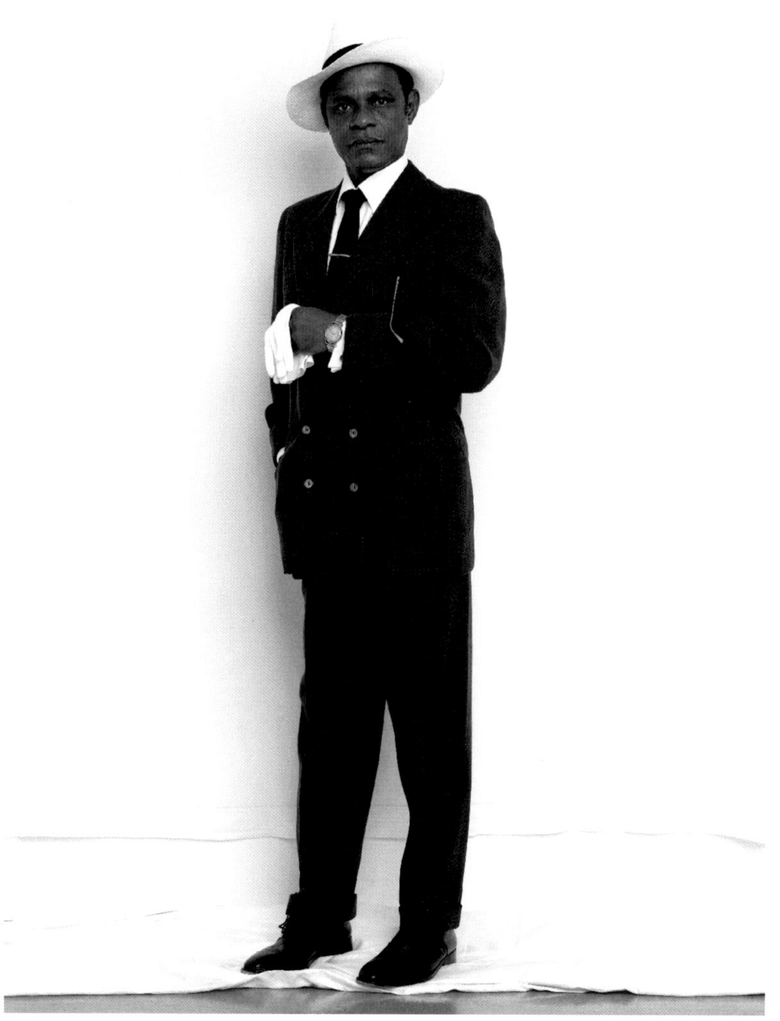

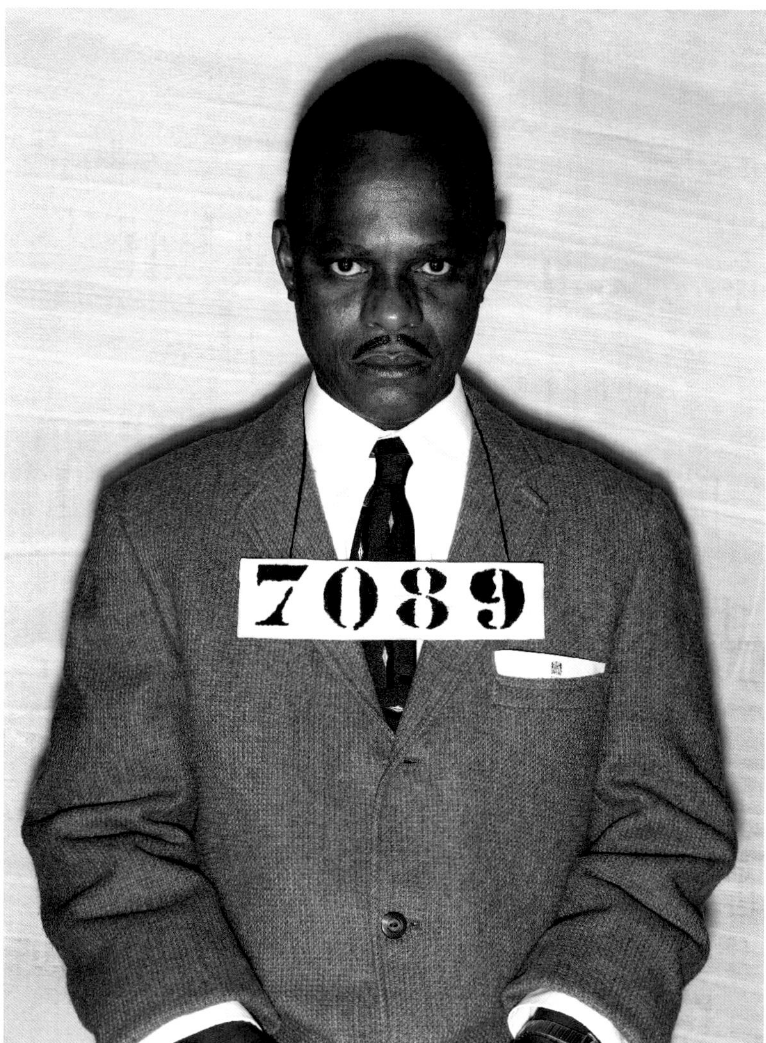

7089

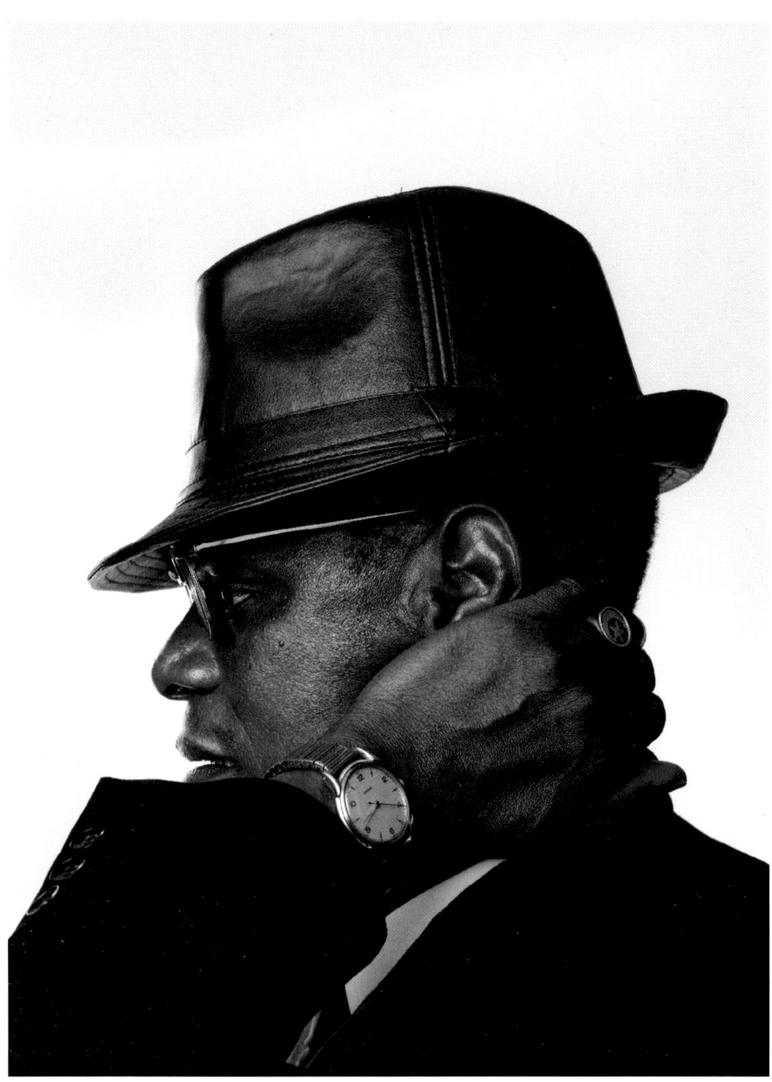

56–59. *Emperor of Africa* series, 2013.

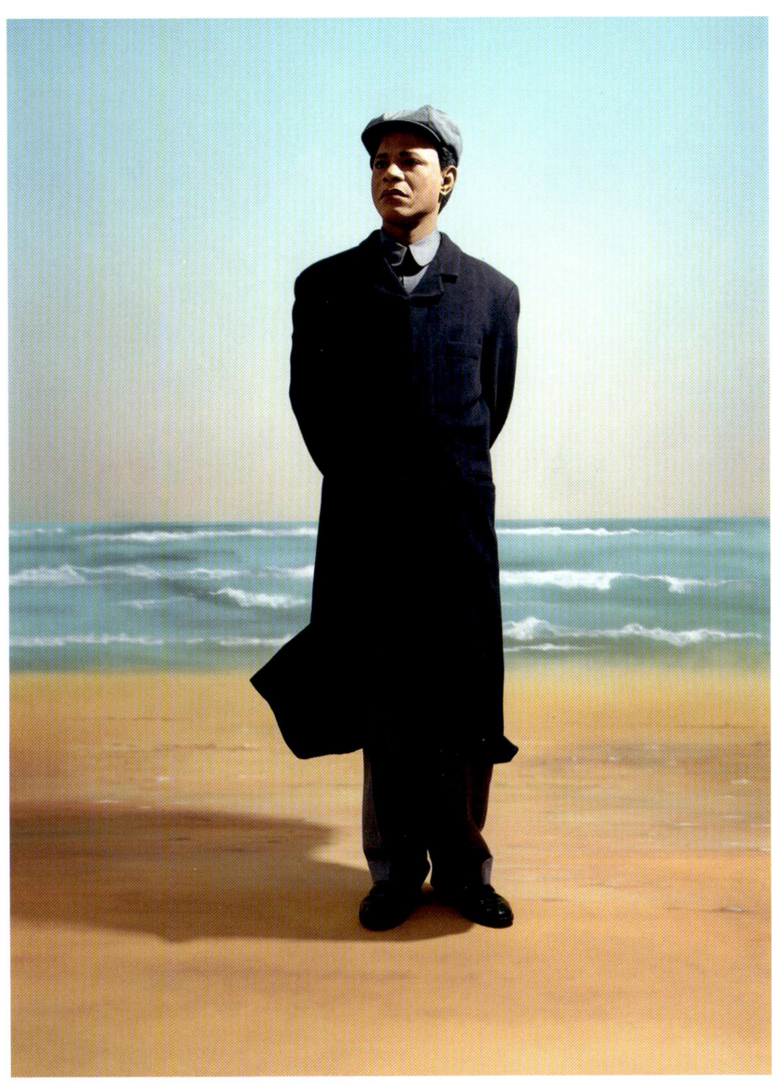

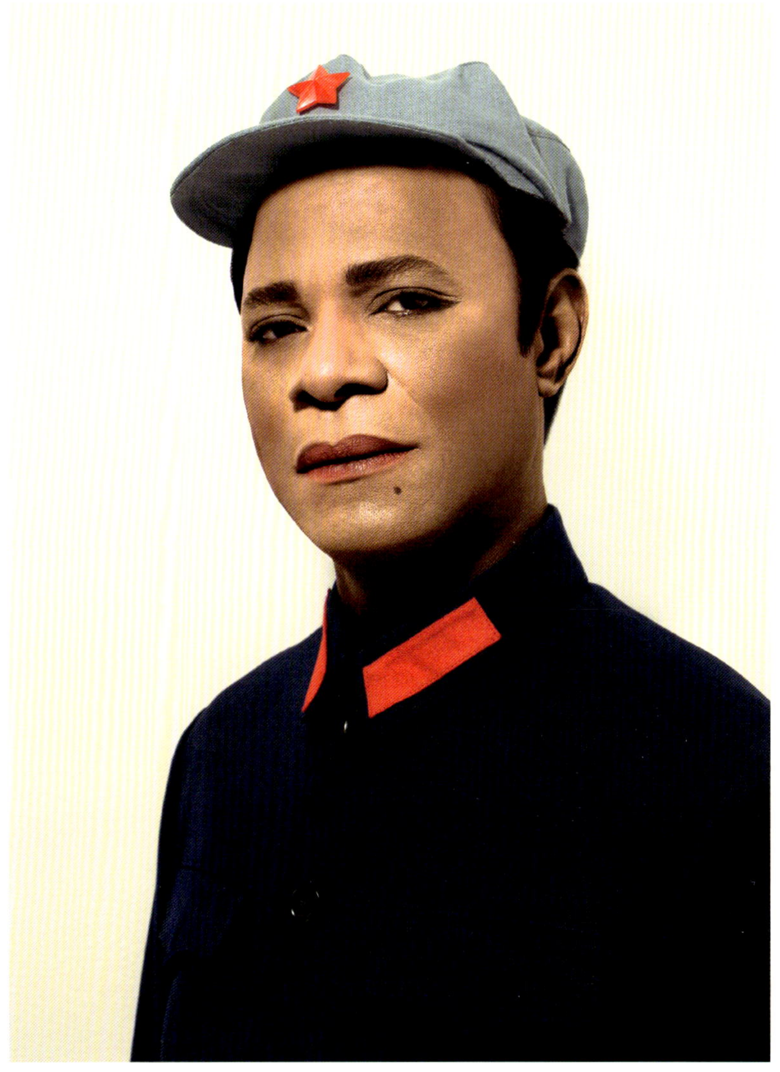

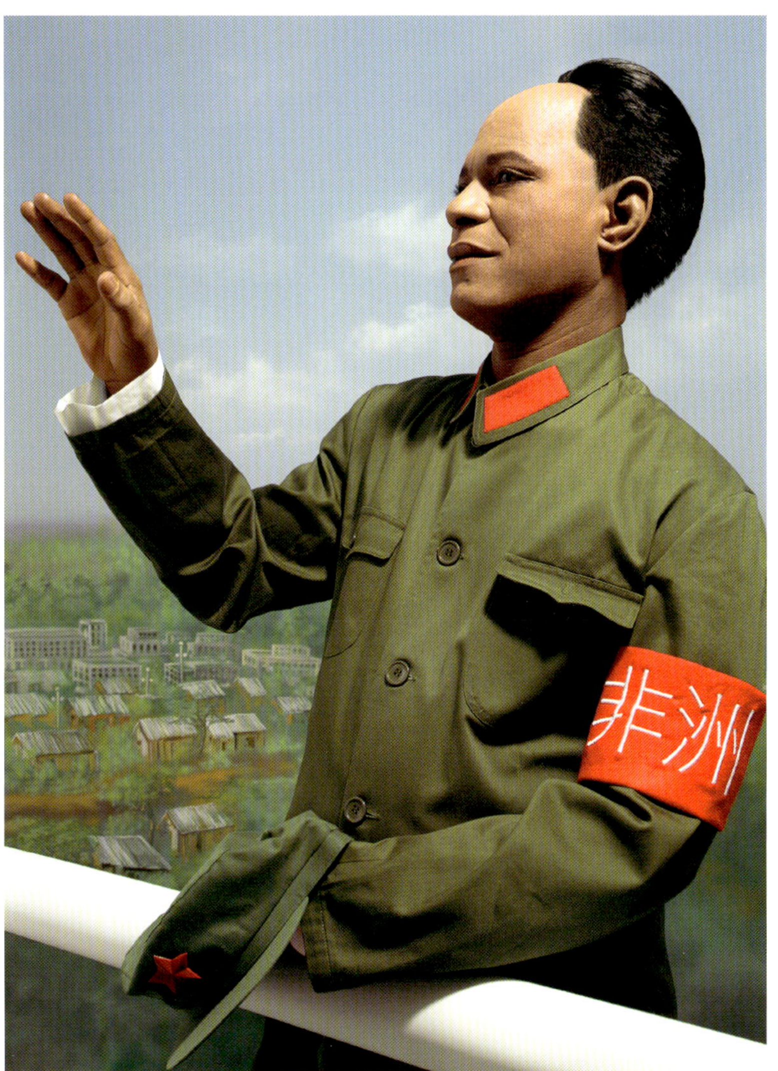

非洲

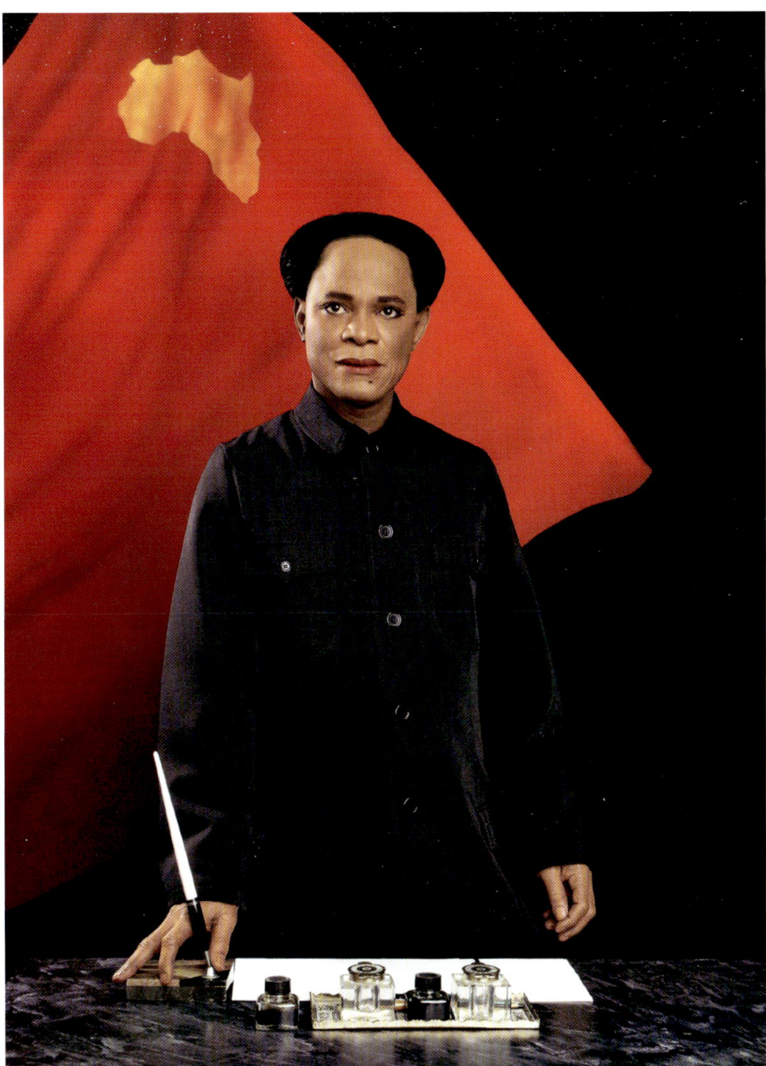

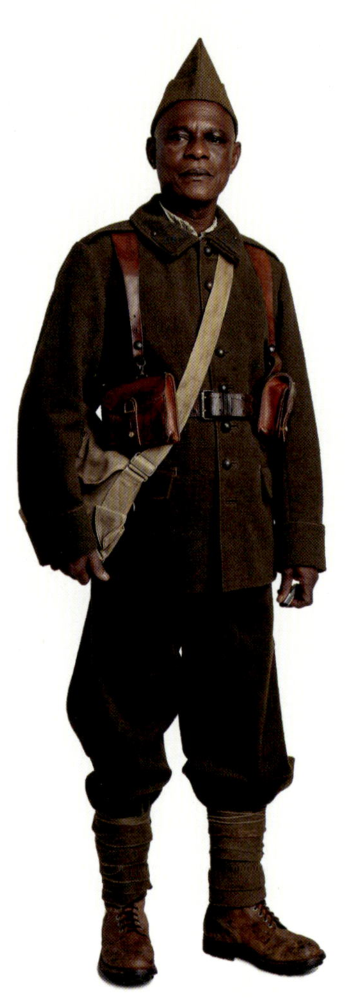

60–61. *ALLONZENFANS* series, 2013.

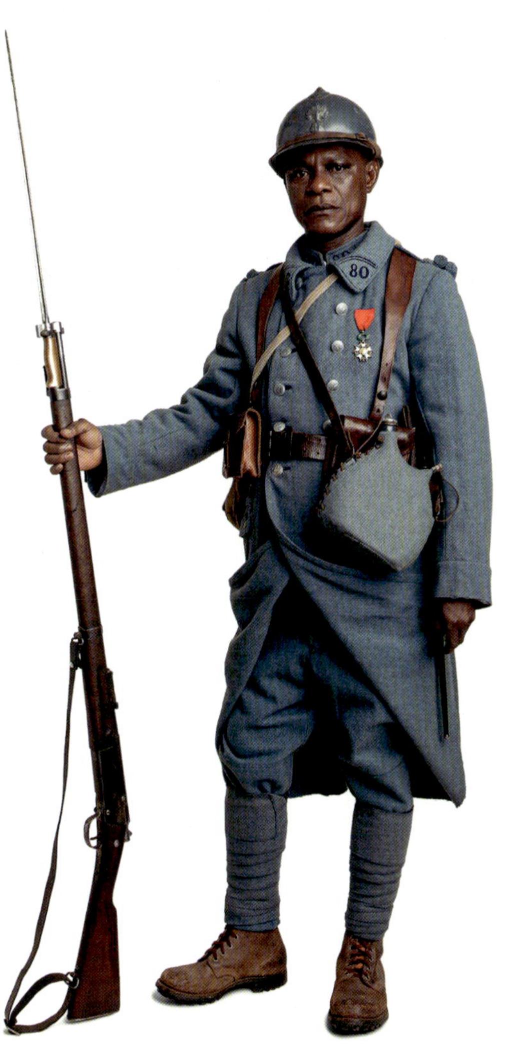

62–81. *SIXSIXSIX* series, 2016. Details.

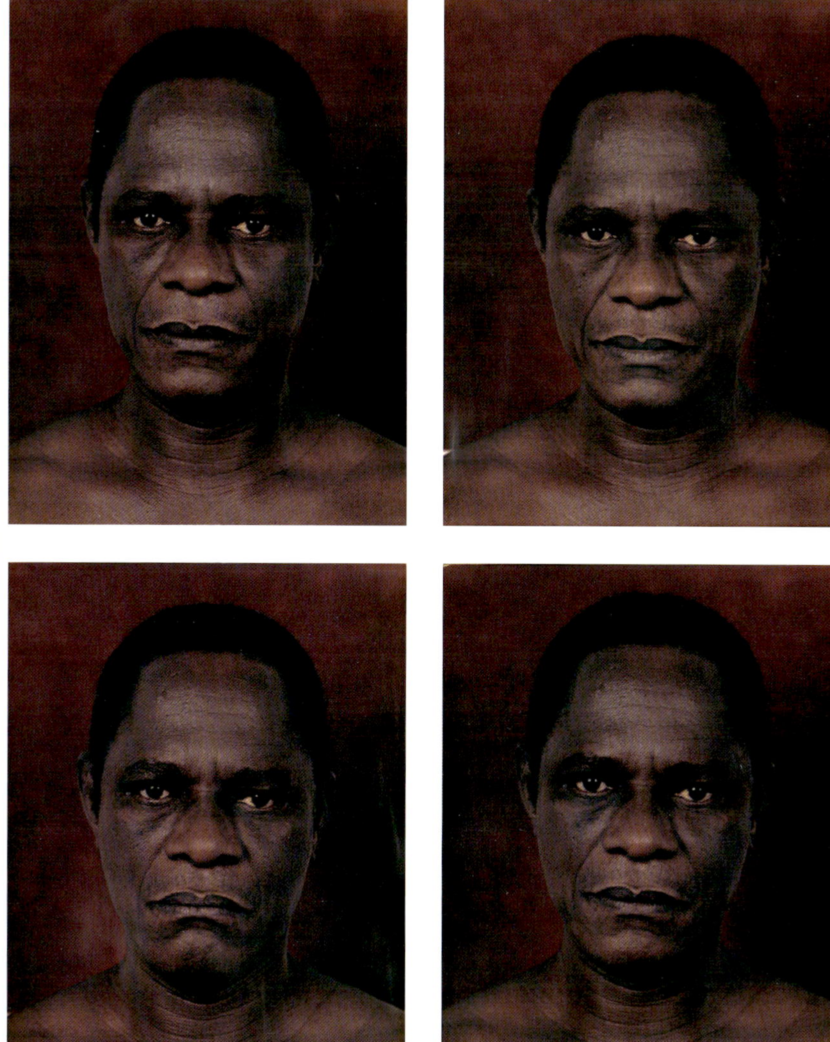

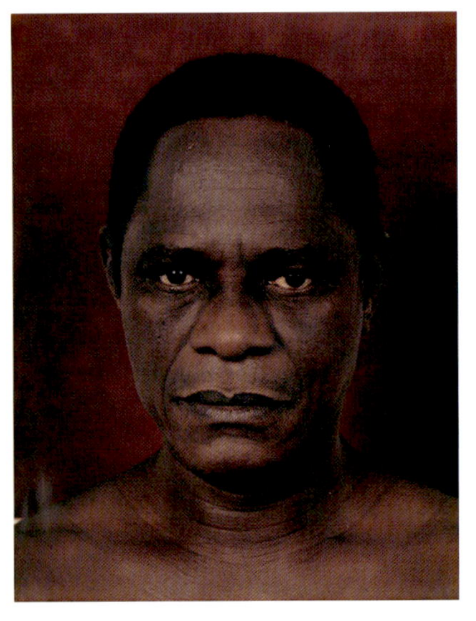
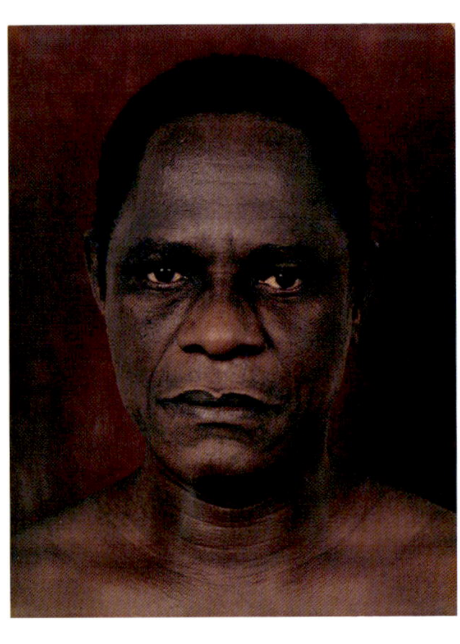
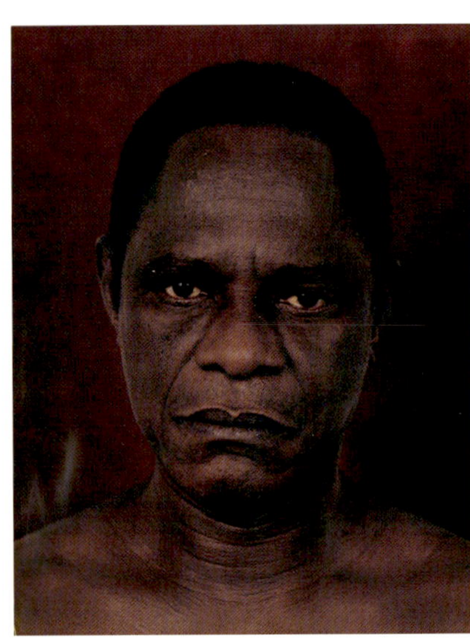
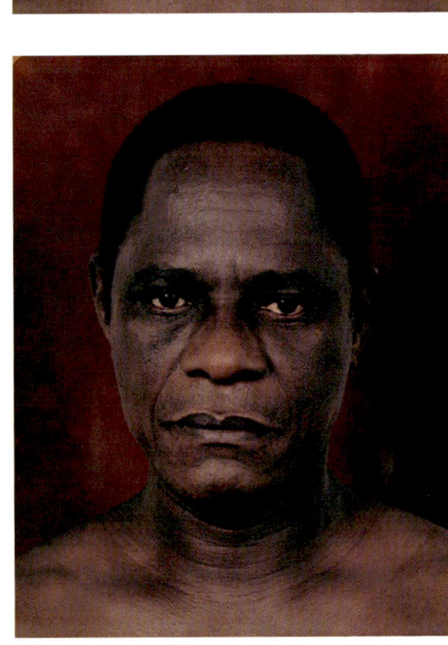

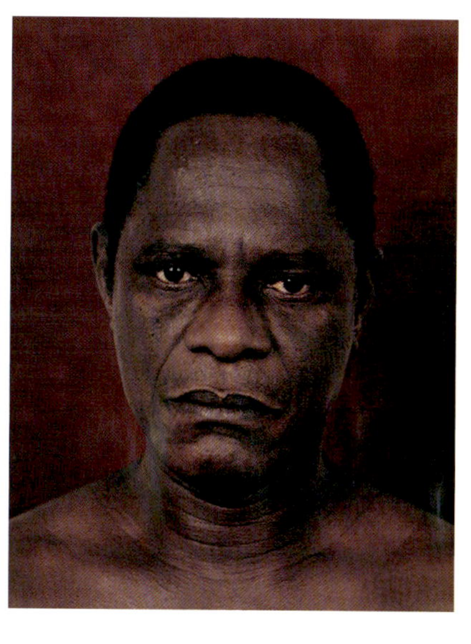
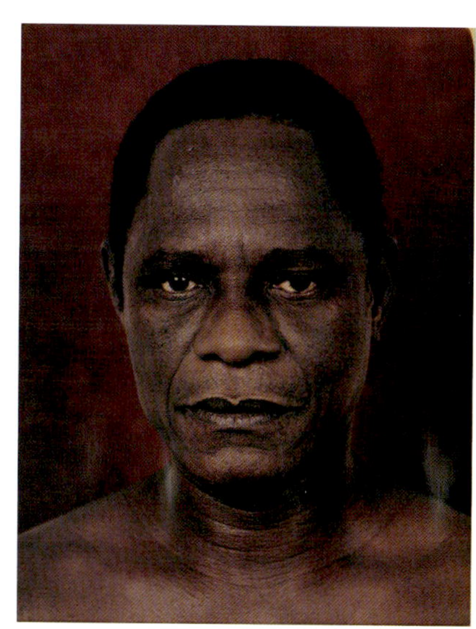
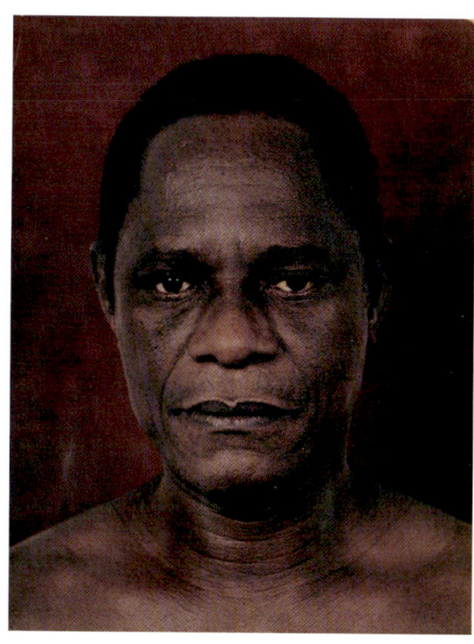
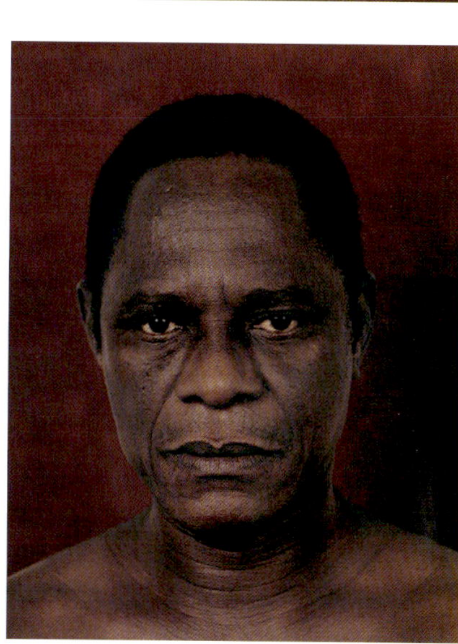

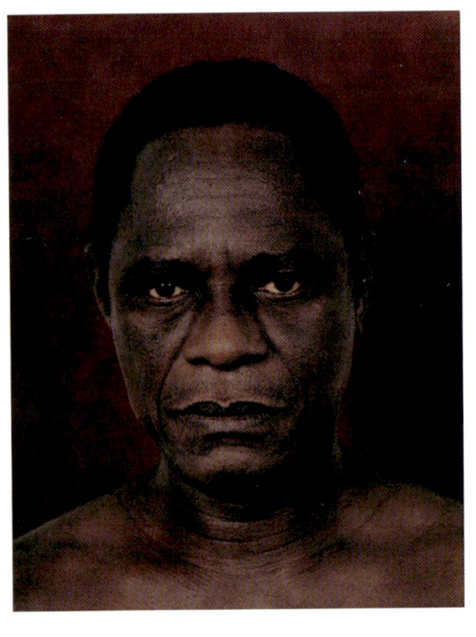
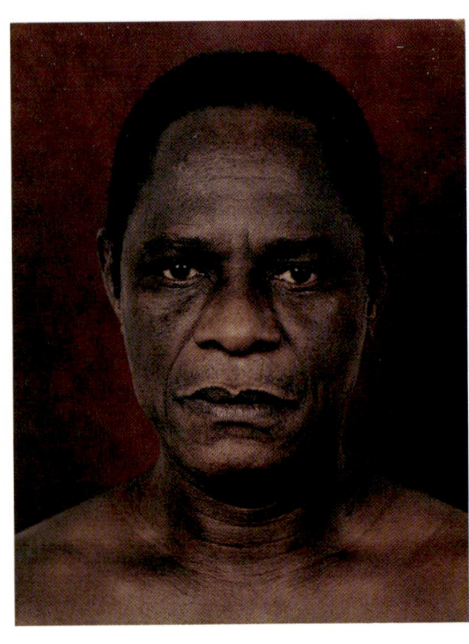
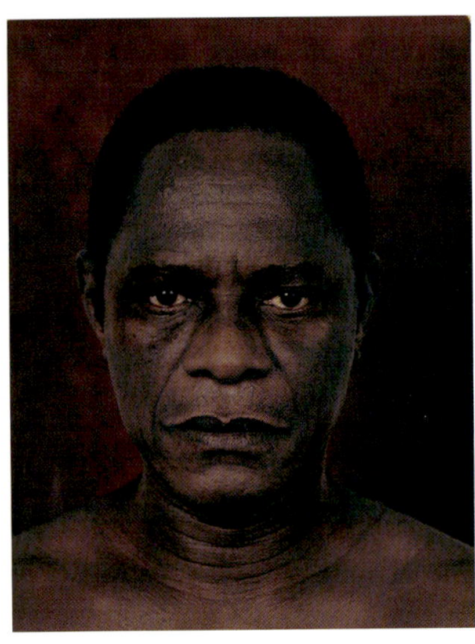
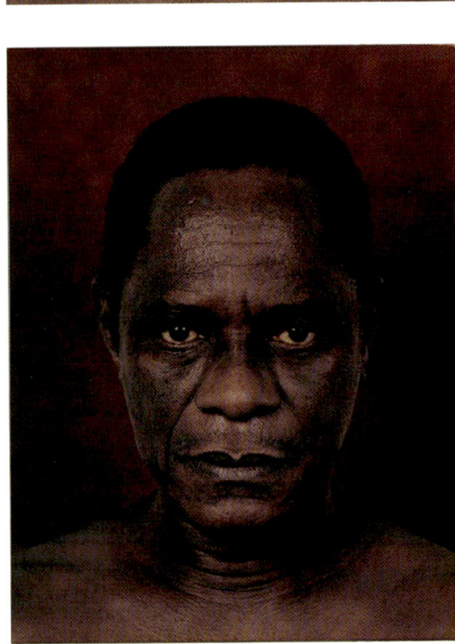

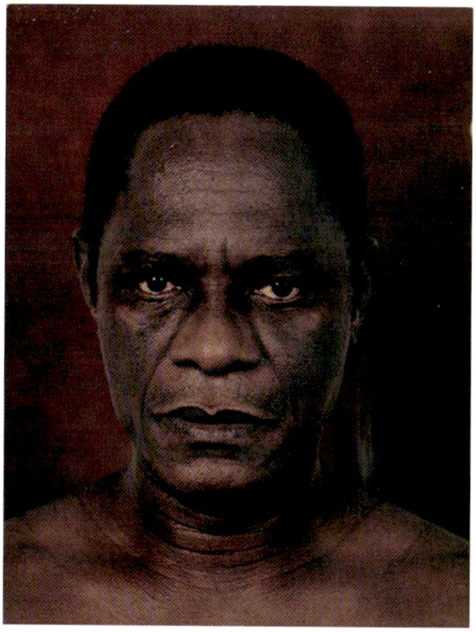

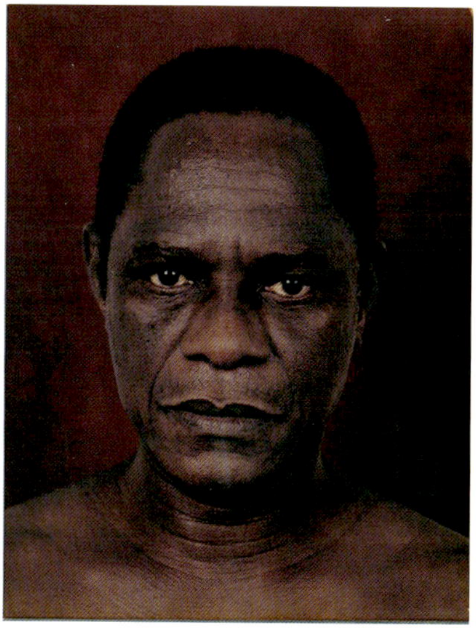

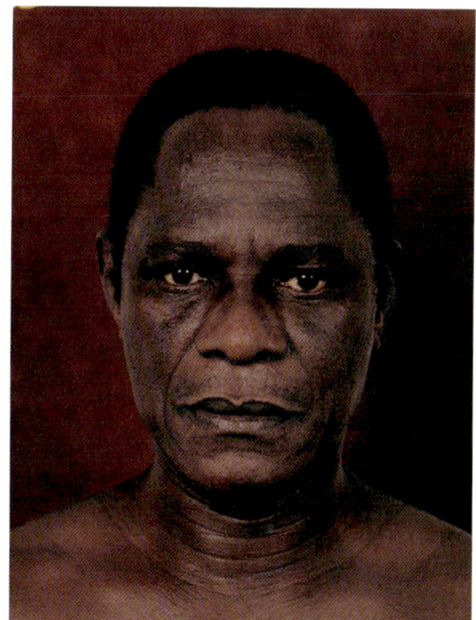
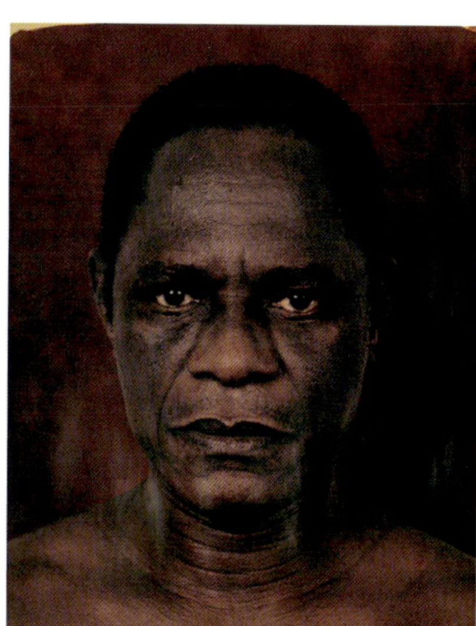

82–85. *Black Pope* series, 2017.

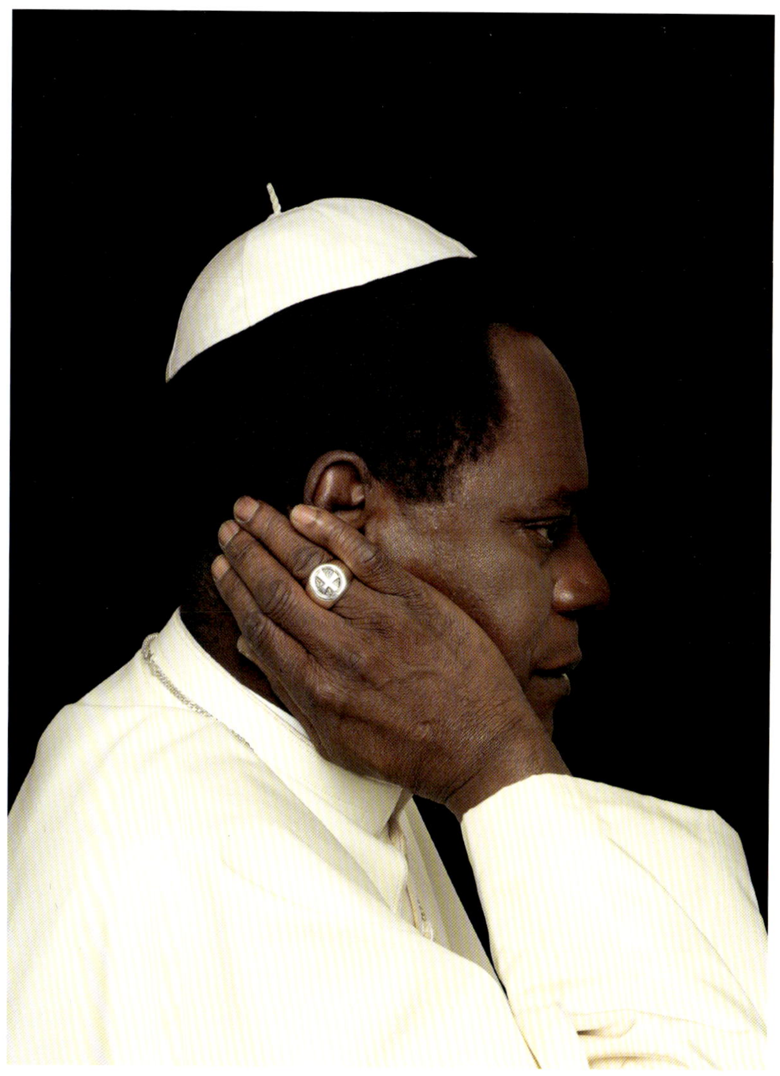

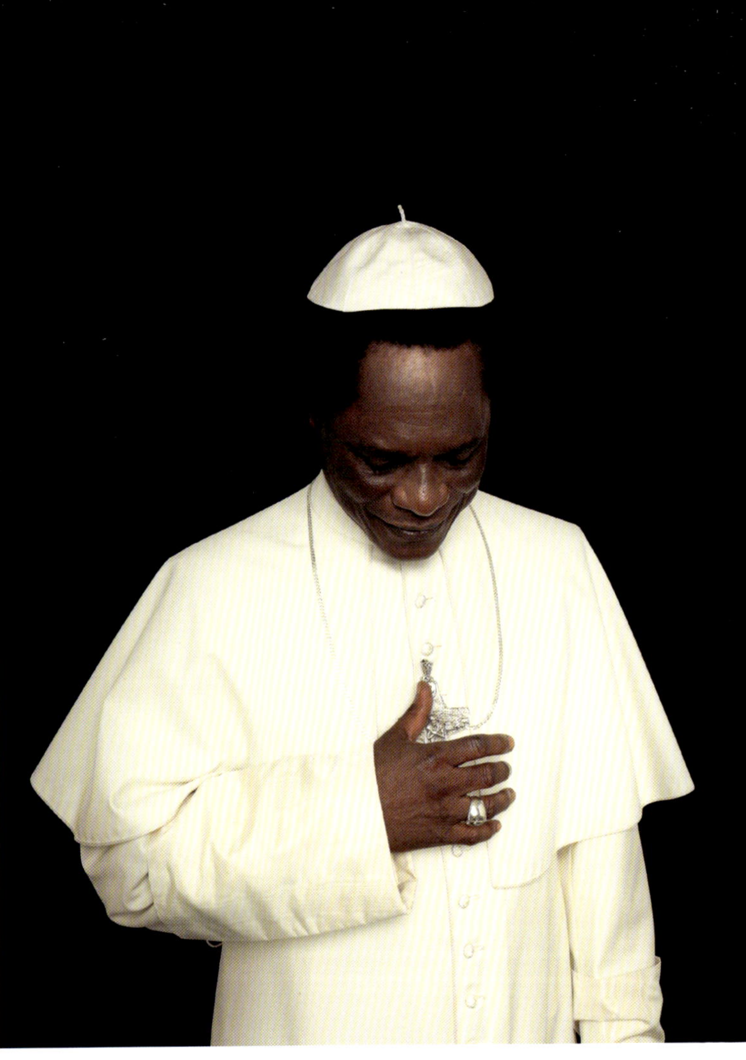

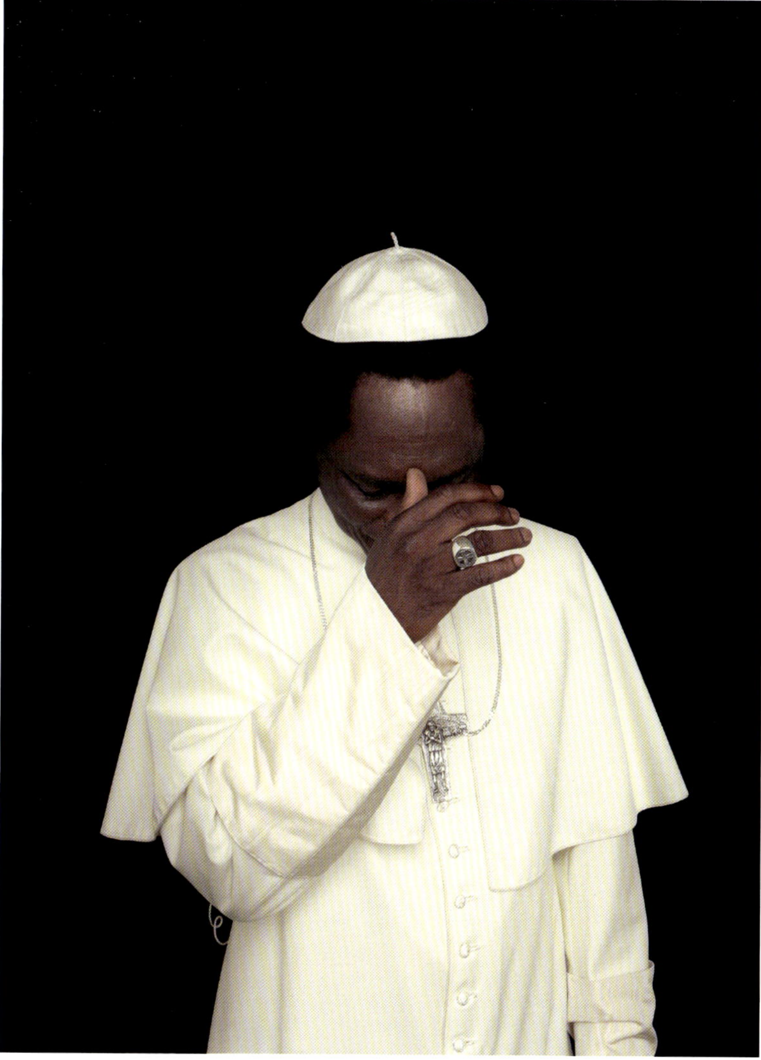

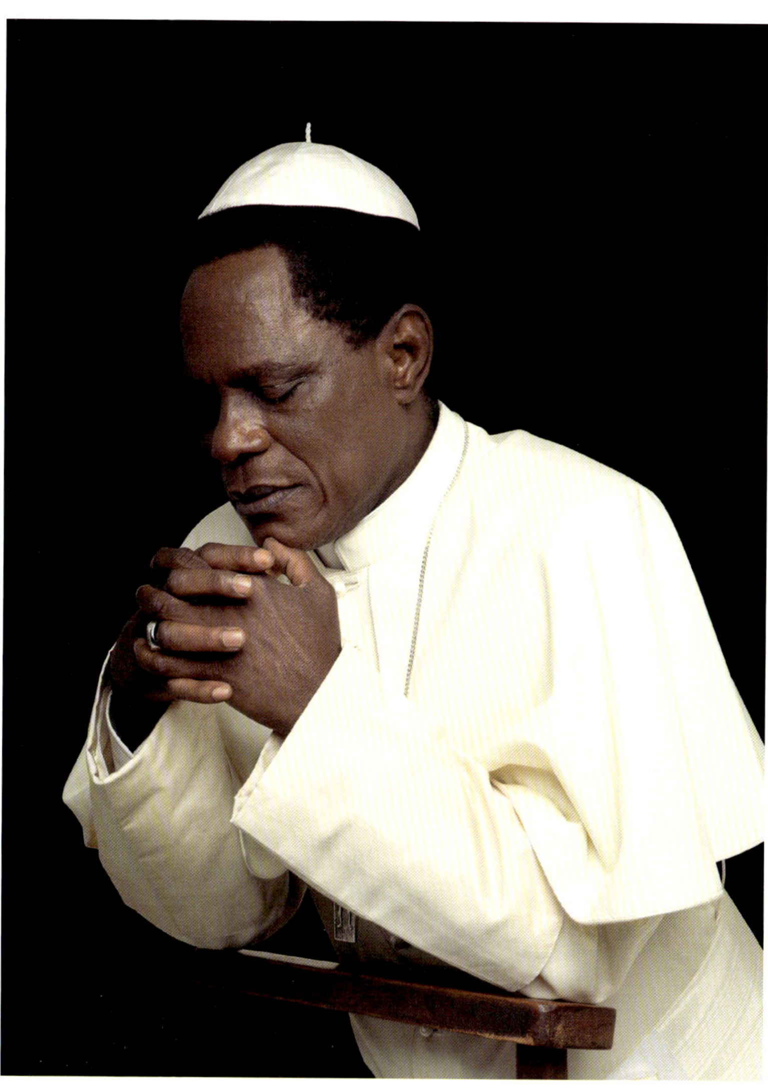

86–87. *Fosso Fashion 2021* series, 2021.

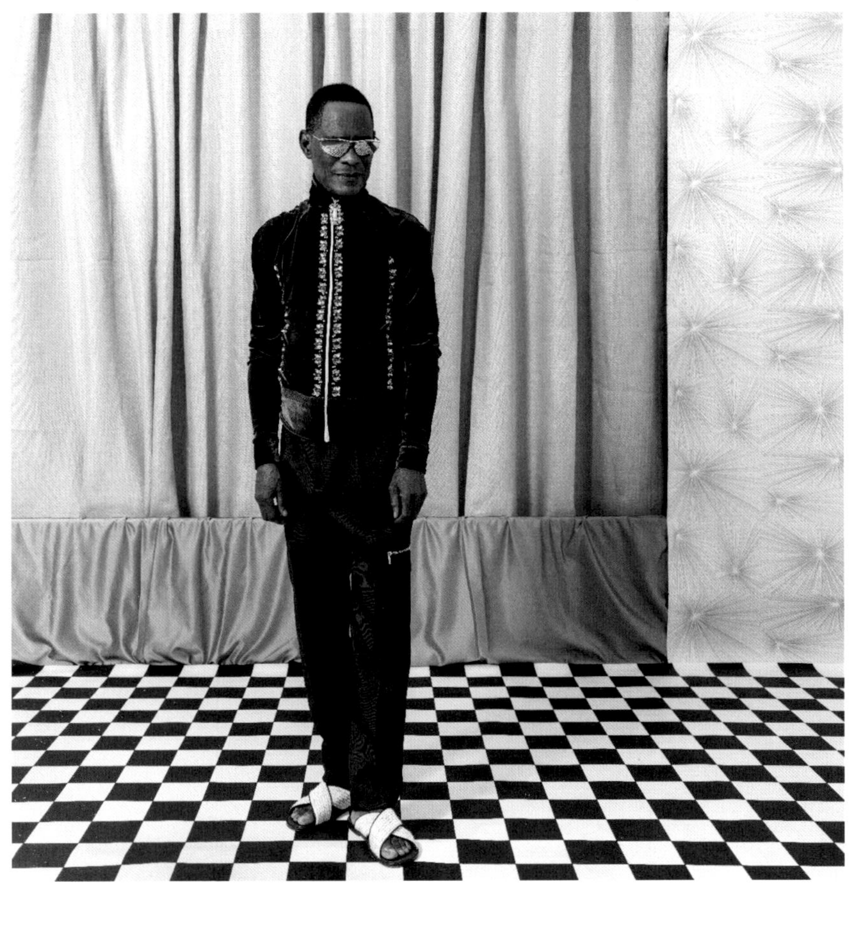

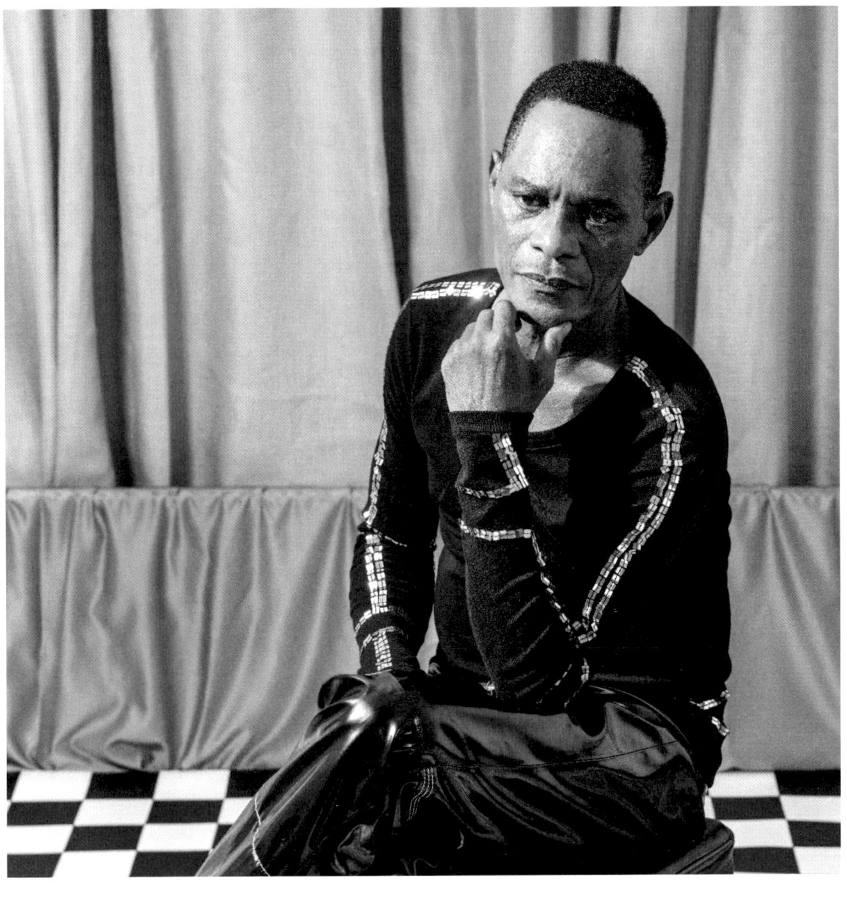

Biography

1962 Born in Kumba, Cameroon.
Suffering from paralysis of the arms and legs,
Samuel Fosso is taken to the Biafra region in
Nigeria, where he is successfully treated by
his grandfather, a healer.

1967 On the outbreak of the Biafran War, the
family flees, spending three years in the
jungle.

1970 After the death of his mother, at the end of
the war, he returns to Edda in Nigeria with his
grandparents.

1972 One of his uncles takes him to Bangui, in
the Central African Republic, to be trained as
a shoemaker.

1974 He starts an apprenticeship at the Tonatus
photography studio in Bangui, and carries out
small jobs. He shoots his first self-portrait.

1975 In March, he starts taking photographs
at the Tonatus studio and in September opens
his own studio, the Studio Photo Nationale,
in the Km5 district. He begins to take self-
portraits alongside his commercial work.

1976 He opens a second studio in the Miskin
district in Bangui, the Studio Confiance, which
becomes Studio Gentil in 1977, then Studio
Hobereau in 1979, and Studio Convenance
from 1982.

1980 He creates Highlight, a sister business
near his studio, with a photographer who
makes films while he himself makes prints.
At the end of the 1980s, the advancement of
colour technology means competition for
studios using traditional black and white.
He continues to sell photography products
and photocopiers.

1993 He meets Bernard Descamps who
discovers the self-portraits he has created.

1994 First exhibition of his *Autoportrait* series
at the Bamako Biennale, curated by Françoise
Huguier and Bernard Descamps.

1995 His *Autoportraits* are exhibited at the
Centre National de la Photographie in Paris,
alongside work by Martin Parr and Marie-
Paule Nègre. He receives encouragement
from Henri Cartier-Bresson. He is awarded
the Afrique en Création prize and begins
to gain international recognition through
numerous exhibitions. From 1995 to 1999,
he is represented by the Galerie Maï Ollivier.

1997 For a commission from the Tati
department store, he shoots the *Tati* series.

1999 He produces the *Fosso Fashion* series.
From 2000, he is represented by the art agent
Jean Marc Patras.

2000 He creates *Mémoire d'un ami* and
receives first prize for photography at the
Dak'Art Biennale in Senegal.

2001 He receives the Prince Claus Fund
Award in the Netherlands.

2003 He produces the series *Le Rêve de mon
grand-père*.

2008 He produces the *African Spirits* series.

2013 He produces the *Emperor of Africa* and
ALLONZENFANS series.

2014 His studio in Bangui is looted during the civil war in the Central African Republic.

2016 He produces *SIXSIXSIX*.

2017 He produces the *Black Pope* series.

2018 He receives the ICP Infinity Award in the Art category and the PHotoESPAÑA Award.

2019 He is made a Chevalier de l'Ordre des Arts et des Lettres.

2021 He produces the *Fosso Fashion 2021* series, in collaboration with fashion designer Grace Wales Bonner.

Selected Bibliography

1996 *In/sight: African Photographers, 1940 to the Present*, texts by Clare Bell, Okwui Enwezor, Olu Oguibe and Octavio Zaya, Guggenheim Museum, New York

1998 *Tati 50/50*, Steidl, Göttingen

– *Anthologie de la photographie africaine et de l'océan Indien*, Revue Noire, Paris

2000 'Fosso Fashion' in *Vogue Hommes* no. 6, Autumn/Winter 1999–2000, Paris

– *Porträt Afrika: Fotografische Positionen eines Jahrhunderts*, catalogue, Haus der Kulturen der Welt, Berlin

2001 *The Short Century: Independence and Liberation Movements in Africa, 1945–1994*, Prestel, Munich

– *Africas. The Artist and the City. A Journey and an Exhibition*, Actar, Barcelona

– *Africa Inside*, Aurora Borealis, Groningen

– *Different*, Stuart Hall and Mark Sealy, Phaidon Press, London

2004 *Samuel Fosso*, text by Maria Francesca Bonetti and Guido Schlinkert, 5 Continents Editions, Milan

2005 *Africa Remix: l'art contemporain d'un continent*, Éditions du Centre Pompidou, Paris

2006 *Masquerade: Representation and the Self in Contemporary Art*, text by Rachel Kent, Museum of Contemporary Art, Sydney

2007 *Collection photographies: une histoire de la photographie à travers les collections du Centre Pompidou*, text by Clément Chéroux, Musée National d'Art Moderne, Éditions du Centre Pompidou, Paris

2009 *Contemporary African Art Since 1980*, text by Okwui Enwezor and Chika Okeke-Agulu, Damiani, Bologna

2010 *Samuel Fosso: Dorian Gray à Bangui*, text by Simon Njami, Revue Noire, Paris

– *Contemporary African Photography from The Walther Collection*, with contributions by Okwui Enwezor (ed.) et al., Steidl, Göttingen

2014 *The Image of the Black in Western Art, Volume V: The Twentieth Century, Part 2: The Rise of Black Artists*, edited by David Bindman and Henry Louis Gates, Jr, Harvard University Press, Cambridge (MA)

2015 *Samuel Fosso: Emperor of Africa*, text by Olu Oguibe, *Aperture*, no. 221, New York

2016 *Performing for the Camera*, edited by Simon Baker and Fiontan Moran, Tate Publishing, London

2017 'The Lives of Samuel Fosso.
A Conversation with Yves Chatap', *Aperture*,
no. 227, Summer, New York
– *Le Métier de photographe en Afrique: 10 ans
d'Afrique in visu*, Maison CF, Paris
– *Being a Photographer in Africa: the 10 Years
of Afrique in visu*, text 'In the style of Samuel
Fosso' by Jeanne Mercier, Maison CF, Paris
– *The Image of the Black in African and Asian Art*,
edited by David Bindman, Suzanne Preston Blier
and Henry Louis Gates, Jr, The Belknap Press
of Harvard University Press, Cambridge (MA)/
London
2019 *La Voix du voir. Les grands entretiens
de la Fondation Henri Cartier-Bresson*, text
'Samuel Fosso' by Clément Chéroux, Éditions
Xavier Barral, Paris
– *MoMA Highlights: 375 Works from The
Museum of Modern Art*, edited by Rebecca
Roberts with Dawn Chan, Kamilah
Foreman, Emily Hall and Diana Stoll,
MoMA Publications, New York
2020 *Samuel Fosso: SIXSIXSIX*, with a
conversation between Samuel Fosso and
Hans Ulrich Obrist, Steidl/The Walther
Collection, New York
– *Samuel Fosso: Autoportrait*, edited by
Okwui Enwezor, contributions by Quentin
Bajac, Yves Chatap, Elvira Dyangani Ose,
Chika Okeke-Agulu, Oluremi C. Onabanjo,
Jean Marc Patras, Terry Smith, Claire
Staebler, James Thomas and Artur Walther,
Steidl/The Walther Collection, New York
– *A toi appartient le regard et [...] la liaison
infinie entre les choses*, edited by Christine
Barthe, Musée du Quai Branly – Jacques
Chirac/Actes Sud, Arles
2021 'Autoportraits II (Fosso Fashion 2021)',
A Magazine Curated by Grace Wales Bonner,
Paris

Selected Exhibitions

Solo Exhibitions
1994 'Autoportraits', 1st Rencontres Africaines
de la Photographie, Bamako
1995 Centre National de la Photographie,
Paris
1996 Galerie du Théâtre, Gap
– Artothèque de Grenoble
1997 'Samuel Fosso: Photographs',
Greengrassi Gallery, London; L'Abattoir,
Chalon-sur-Saône
1999 Galerie Maï Ollivier, Paris
2003 'Samuel Fosso', Jack Shainman Gallery,
New York
– 'Autorretratos', PHotoEspaña, Madrid
2004 'Samuel Fosso', Istituto Centrale
per la Grafica, Rome; Centro Internazionale
di Fotografia Scavi Scaligeri, Verona
2005 'Autoportraits', Platform for Art,
Gloucester Road Underground Station,
London
2007 'Samuel Fosso. Monographie',
7th Rencontres Africaines de la
Photographie, Bamako
– 'Samuel Fosso, Vol. II (*Tati* series)', Galerie
Jean Marc Patras, Paris

– 'Samuel Fosso, Vol. I (*Le Rêve de mon grand-père* series)', Galerie Jean Marc Patras, Paris

2008 'African Spirits', Galerie Jean Marc Patras, Paris

– 'Autoportraits', Photoink, New Delhi

– 'Autorretratos', Festival de la Luz, Maman Fine Art Gallery, Buenos Aires

– 'Vous serez beau, chic, délicat et facile à reconnaître. Autoportraits. Sélection de Christian Lacroix', Les Ateliers des Forges, 39th Rencontres de la Photographie d'Arles, Arles

2010 '30 ans d'autoportraits', Maison des Arts et de la Culture, Créteil

– 'Samuel Fosso, autoportraits 1970–2008', Institut Français, Dakar; N'Djamena; Harare; Bulawayo; Antananarivo

2013 'Samuel Fosso', Purdy Hicks Gallery, London

– 'Samuel Fosso: African Spirits, The Emperor of Africa', 4th LagosPhoto Festival, Lagos

2014 'Samuel Fosso', The Walther Collection Project Space, New York

2015 'Looting/Pillage', Paris Photo, Galerie Jean Marc Patras, Paris

2017 'Transitions: Samuel Fosso dans la collection du FRAC Réunion', Maison Bédier, Piton Saint-Leu

– 'Samuel Fosso: Self-Portraits', National Portrait Gallery, London

2018 'Samuel Fosso: An African Odyssey', PHotoEspaña, Fernán Gómez Centro Cultural de la Villa, Madrid

2021–22 'Samuel Fosso', Maison Européenne de la Photographie, Paris

Group Shows

1995 'Photographes africains', FNAC, Forum des Halles, Paris

1996 'In/sight: African Photographers, 1940 to the Present', Guggenheim Museum, New York

– 'Festival des 3 Continents', Nantes

1997 'Studio Photo, 50 ans des magasins Tati', Musée des Arts Décoratifs, Paris

– 'Lumière Noire: Arts Traditionnels', Centre d'Art de Tanlay, Tanlay

– 'Retrats de l'anima. Fotografia Africana', Fundación La Caixa, Barcelona

1998 'L'Afrique par elle-même', Maison Européenne de la Photographie, Paris

1999 'Africa by Africa: A Photographic View', Barbican Art Gallery, London

2000 Dak'Art – Biennale de l'Art Africain Contemporain, Dakar

– 'Africa Inside: Photography from Africa', Noorderlicht Photo Festival, Fries Museum, Leeuwarden; Museokeskus Vapriikki, Tampere

2001 'The Short Century: Independence and Liberation Movements in Africa, 1945–1994', Museum Villa Stuck, Munich; Haus der Kulturen der Welt, Berlin; MoMA PS1, New York; Museum of Contemporary Art, Chicago

– 'Africas: The Artist and the City – A Journey

and an Exhibition', Centre de Cultura
Contemporània de Barcelona

2002 6th International Photography
Gathering, Aleppo

– 'Samuel Fosso, Seydou Keïta, Malick Sidibé:
Portraits of Pride', Xpo September Stockholm
Fotofestival, Moderna Museet c/o Enkehuset,
Stockholm; Bildens Hus, Sundsvall; Preus
Museum, Horten

2003 'Make Life Beautiful! The Dandy in
Photography', Brighton Museum, Brighton

– 'Geometry of the Face: Photographic
Portraits', Det Nationale Fotomuseum,
Copenhagen

2004 26th São Paulo Biennial, São Paulo

– 'Image and Identity: Portraits by Philip
Kwame Apagya, Samuel Fosso, Seydou
Keïta, Malick Sidibé', Sheldon Art Galleries,
St Louis (MO)

– 'Africa Screams', Iwalewahaus Universität
Bayreuth, Bayreuth

– 'Africa Remix', Museum Kunstpalast,
Düsseldorf

2005 'Art That Works/Catch Me!', 46th October
Salon, Belgrade

– 'Africa Remix', Hayward Gallery, London;
Centre Pompidou, Paris

2006 'Masquerade: Representation and the
Self in Contemporary Art', Museum of
Contemporary Art, Sydney

– 'The Whole World is Rotten', Contemporary
Arts Center, Cincinnati (OH)

– 'Expanding Africa: New Art, New Directions',
Newark Museum of Art, Newark (NJ)

2007 'Role Exchange', Sean Kelly Gallery,
New York

– 'Africa Remix', Johannesburg Art Gallery,
Johannesburg

2009 'Unbounded: New Art for a New Century',
Newark Museum, Newark (NJ)

– 'Intimate Geographies', Marcelino Botín
Foundation, Santander

2010 2nd Luanda Triennial, Luanda

– 'Events of the Self: Portraiture and
Social Identity', The Walther Collection,
Neu-Ulm

– 'A Useful Dream: African Photography
1960–2010', Bozar Centre for Fine Arts,
Brussels

2011 'ARS 11', Kiasma Museum of
Contemporary Art, Helsinki

2012 'Ladies and Gentlemen!', Moderna
Museet, Malmö

– 'Africa Africa', Abbaye Saint-André,
Centre d'Art Contemporain, Meymac

– 'L'histoire est à moi', Les Abattoirs, Printemps
de Septembre, Toulouse

– 'Broken Memories', Museu Afro Brasil,
São Paulo

– 'The Progress of Love', Menil Collection,
Houston (TX)

2013 'Distance and Desire: Encounters with
the African Archive', The Walther Collection,
Neu-Ulm

2014 'Typology, Taxonomy, and Seriality:
Photography from The Walther Collection',
45th Rencontres de la Photographie d'Arles,
Arles

2015 'In and Out of the Studio: Photographic Portraits from West Africa', MoMA, New York
– 'You Love Me, You Love Me Not', Fundação Sindika Dokolo, Porto
– 'Après Eden: The Walther Collection', La Maison Rouge, Paris
– 'Folk art africain? Créations contemporaines en Afrique subsaharienne', Frac Aquitaine, Bordeaux
– 'In the Studio: Photographs', Gagosian Gallery, New York
2016 'Made You Look: Dandyism and Black Masculinity', The Photographers' Gallery, London
– 'Où poser la tête?', FRAC Réunion / Institut d'Art Contemporain de l'Océan Indien, Port Louis, Mauritius
– 'The Expanded Subject: New Perspectives in Photographic Portraiture from Africa', Miriam and Ira D. Wallach Art Gallery, Columbia University, New York
– 'Portrait de l'artiste en alter', Frac Haute-Normandie, Sotteville-lès-Rouen
– 'A History. Contemporary Art from the Centre Pompidou', Haus der Kunst, Munich
– 'Performing for the Camera', Tate Modern, London
– 'Françoise Huguier: Regard sur la photographie africaine', Fondation Blachère, Apt
2017 'Afrofuturism: Transhumans Imagining a New Vision for Africa', Galerie Médina, 11th Rencontres Africaines de la Photographie, Bamako; Tropenmuseum, Amsterdam
– 'Chin(A)frica: an interface', James B. Duke House, New York
– 'Regimes of Truth', 8th LagosPhoto Festival, Lagos
– 'What Does the Image Stand For?', MOMENTA/Biennale de l'image, Montreal
– 'After the Fact: Propaganda in the 21st Century', Städtische Galerie im Lenbachhaus und Kunstbau, Munich
– 'Unfinished Conversations: New Work from the Collection', MoMA, New York
– '10 Years Old', Fondazione Fotografia Modena (Fondazione Modena Arti Visive), Modena
– 'When the Heavens Meet the Earth: Selected Works from Robert Devereux's Sina Jina Collection of Contemporary Art', The Heong Gallery at Downing College, Cambridge
2018 'Claude, Samuel, Zanele', Fotomuseum Antwerpen (FOMU), Antwerp
– 'Structures of Identity: Photography from The Walther Collection', Museo Amparo, Puebla; Museo de Arte Contemporáneo de Monterrey (MARCO), Monterrey; Foam Fotografiemuseum, Amsterdam; Foto Colectania, Barcelona
– 'From Africa to the Americas: Face-to-face Picasso, Past and Present', Montreal Museum of Fine Arts, Montreal
– 'Drag: Self-portraits and Body Politics', Hayward Gallery, London
– 'Talisman in the Age of Difference', curated

by Yinka Shonibare MBE, Stephen Friedman
Gallery, London
– 'Mistaken Identities: Images of Gender
and Transformation', The Walther Collection
Project Space, New York
– 'Afriques, artistes d'hier et d'aujourd'hui',
Fondation Clément, Le François, Martinique
2019 'Age of You', Museum of Contemporary
Art, Toronto
– 'Here We are Today: Das Bild der Welt in
Foto- & Videokunst', Bucerius Kunst Forum,
Hamburg
– 'Artistic License: Six Takes on the
Guggenheim Collection', Guggenheim
Museum, New York
– 'Changing Views: 20 Years of Art Collection
Deutsche Börse', Foam Fotografiemuseum,
Amsterdam
– 'Encore: Reenactment in Contemporary
Photography', J. Paul Getty Museum at the
Getty Center, Los Angeles
– 'Your Mirror: Portraits from the ICP
Collection', International Center of
Photography, New York
2020 'African Cosmologies: Photography,
Time, and the Other', FotoFest Biennial,
Houston (TX)
– 'Staging Identity', Institut Mathildenhöhe,
Darmstadt
– 'Crossing Views. La Collection, regards sur
un nouveau choix d'œuvres', Fondation
Louis Vuitton, Paris
– 'À toi appartient le regard et [...] la liaison
infinie entre les choses', Musée du Quai
Branly – Jacques Chirac, Paris
– 'Masculinities: Liberation through
Photography', Barbican Art Gallery, London
– 'The Cindy Sherman Effect: Identity and
Transformation in Contemporary Art',
Kunstforum Wien, Vienna
2021 'neuf-3. Un projet d'art public à Saint-
Denis', Saint-Denis
– 'This World is White No Longer. Views of
a Decentered World', Museum der Moderne
Salzburg, Salzburg
– 'Masculinities: Liberation through
Photography', Martin Gropius Bau,
Berlin; LUMA Arles, Arles; FOMU, Antwerp
2022 'Look at Me: Photography from The
Walther Collection', K21, Kunstsammlung
Nordrhein-Westfalen, Düsseldorf
– 'African Cosmologies Redux', FotoFest
Biennial, Houston (TX)

The Photofile series is the original English-language
edition of the Photo Poche collection. It was first published
between 1986 and 1992 by the Centre National de la
Photographie, Paris, with the support of the French
Ministry of Culture. Robert Delpire (1926–2017) was the
creator of the series and its managing editor until 2017.

Series design by Matthew Young

Translated from the French by Ruth Taylor

First published in the United Kingdom in 2022 by
Thames & Hudson Ltd, 181A High Holborn,
London WC1V 7QX

First published in the United States of America
in 2022 by
Thames & Hudson Inc., 500 Fifth Avenue,
New York, New York 10110

British Library Cataloguing-in-Publication Data
A catalogue record for this book is available from
the British Library

Library of Congress Control Number 2021949692

ISBN 978-0-500-41120-9

Printed and bound in Italy